T0345127

# Hardware-Based Computer Security Techniques to Defeat Hackers

# Hardware-Based Computer Security Techniques to Defeat Hackers

## From Biometrics to Quantum Cryptography

**Roger Dube**

**WILEY**

A JOHN WILEY & SONS, INC., PUBLICATION

Published by John Wiley & Sons, Inc., Hoboken, New Jersey.
Published simultaneously in Canada.

For general information on our other products and services or for technical support, please contact our Customer Care Department within the United States at (800) 762-2974, outside the United States at (317) 572-3993 or fax (317) 572-4002.

Wiley also publishes its books in a variety of electronic formats. Some content that appears in print may not be available in electronic format. For information about Wiley products, visit our web site at www.wiley.com.

*Library of Congress Cataloging-in-Publication Data is available.*

ISBN 978-0-470-19339-6

Printed in the United States of America.

10 9 8 7 6 5 4 3 2 1

This book is dedicated to my wife, Jeri, whose undying support and love have given me the courage to chart new directions in my life. The book is also dedicated to my children—Dawn, Danielle, Laura, and Jordan—and their wonderful children as well. The thrill of seeing each of them grow to find their talents, passions and partners in art, science, animal care and writing continues to make life fulfilling. I am very proud of them all.

Finally, the dedication would be incomplete without my deepest thanks to my mom and dad who created and maintained a nurturing environment through easy and hard times alike.

# ACKNOWLEDGMENTS

I would like to express sincere appreciation to a number of professional colleagues who aided in my education as a physicist and my immersive education in the computer security field. The Experimental General Relativity Group at Princeton provided an environment in which a young physicist could learn fundamental approaches to difficult weak signal detection problems. Bill Wickes, the late Dave Wilkinson, Jim Peebles, and Ed Groth provided engaging and challenging discussions on various aspects of differential and phase sensitive detection. My years at IBM Research provided first hand management experience of technology development and commercialization projects, giving me an appreciation of the need to integrate technology and science with product schedules. Omesh Sahni was instrumental in helping me grow as a manager, carefully guiding me through progressively more difficult management situations. At DAT, Rick Morgenstern, Mary Ann Voreck, Peter Patsis, John Burdick, Bill Kazis, and Mukesh Kumar have provided support, companionship and boundless energy as the team worked to develop, refine, and deliver military grade authentication technology to various governmental organizations.

The fine folks at the United States Joint Forces Command, especially the Joint Experimentation Lab headed by Tony Cerri, were helpful, instructive, and patient as our technology was exposed to demanding attacks and attempts to break the hardware-based authentication system that we had developed. Lt. Col. Dave Robinson and Brad Mabe at SAIC invested countless hours helping us test, debug, and refine the technology.

I would like to thank Paul Petralia, senior editor at Wiley, for supporting the concept of the book. Finally, I would like to express my sincerest thanks to Lt. Col. Dave Robinson, who patiently read drafts and offered valuable suggestions, corrections, and refinements even through the height of Michigan football season.

# ABOUT THE AUTHOR

Roger Dube received his bachelor's degree in physics and math from Cornell University and his Ph.D. in experimental physics from Princeton University. He completed a post-doctoral position at Kitt Peak National Observatory in Tucson, where he continued his work on using weak signal detection techniques to tackle problems in experimental general relativity. Over the next few years he held various academic positions at Caltech/Jet Propulsion Laboratory, the University of Michigan, and the University of Arizona. He joined IBM's Research Division in Yorktown Heights, NY after developing a system to store real time data in photorefractive crystals using holography. Dr. Dube rose through management levels at IBM while maintaining an adjunct professorship at nearby Yale University, where he mentored graduate students as well as lectured on device physics and technology commercialization.

Dr. Dube left IBM in 1996 to become president of Gate Technologies International, Inc. (later named Digital Authentication Technologies, Inc.) based in Boca Raton, FL. Gate provided advanced technology search services for leading technology companies in a variety of industries through the year 2000. During those years, it became apparent to Dr. Dube that there was a strong need for a computer security and authentication technology that employed an unalterable physical process as a source of randomness for cryptographic keys. During 2000 and early 2001, Dr. Dube invented the fundamental patents for a physics-based location aware security and authentication technology. Over the course of the next few years, the company received numerous contracts and research grants for the technology to examine how it might be applied to problems of securing information sharing, wireless communication, and control of critical infrastructure.

Dr. Dube currently holds a joint position as president and chief scientist of Digital Authentication Technologies, Inc. and as a professor of imaging science at Rochester Institute of Technology (RIT).

# CONTENTS

**11  A CLOSER LOOK AT BIOMETRICS**                              **147**

# PREFACE

Advances in computer security technologies are occurring at a fast pace. As a result, defenses (over time) are dynamic and forever evolving. As new protective measures appear, new attacks are developed to defeat them, leading to corrective improvements in the protective measures, new attacks, and so on. Hacker organizations, often formed with the intent of forcing developers to improve and harden the security features of their products, meet frequently to discuss new security technologies as well as new attack tools. Challenges and contests in which participants try to break security products or operating systems are mounted frequently and the results published broadly, often to the consternation of the product developer. As more applications migrate to open source, the opportunity for deeper testing of security features is enhanced.

By its very nature, any book on the topic of computer security will be a snapshot of current protection technologies and common attack approaches. For example, even as this book goes to press, new articles are appearing on a possible vulnerability of quantum cryptography, which to date has been considered unbreakable by the intelligence community. Of course, the assertion will be studied and tested by countless groups around the world, and will likely result in an improvement.

With this dynamic quality in mind, readers should review each of the technologies discussed in this book periodically to determine if enhancements or fundamental changes have been made since the time of publishing. New technologies will appear as well, and they need to be subjected to careful analysis and testing before being deployed on mission critical systems. That having been said, the basic physics, mathematics, and electronics that are used to build these technologies do not change, and so the core principles remain the same. The specific implementations are usually the elements that evolve.

The book has been designed to present each security technology from a fundamental principles perspective first, so that the reader can understand the issue that motivated the creation of the technology. With this in mind, the subsequent analysis of the technology's ability to meet those goals and withstand attacks is generally easier to accomplish. Perhaps as important, such an understanding will help a user appreciate the need to implement each technology properly so that the intent of the developers is preserved. Otherwise, additional vulnerabilities due to mismatching interdependencies may be introduced that compromise a specific implementation.

Dependencies are another important aspect of security elements in an information processing environment. No single product is developed without attention to other components or critical processes upon which it depends. Failure of IT administrators to understand such dependencies can undermine a security rollout.

Moreover, as specific security technology elements are broken, awareness of the impact on other elements within a deployment must be evaluated immediately to determine if the entire system is now compromised.

Security administrators must establish early on which priorities override others. For example, in high security organizational systems, control of access or knowledge of employee activities may override privacy of employees. It is important that policy governing these priorities be established early and communicated broadly throughout the organization so that implementations meet the requirements and that employee expectations are not misplaced.

Implementations, interdependencies, specific (existing and new) security technologies and organizational security goals should be revisited annually to assure that mission critical systems continue to be protected to the highest level possible. A fresh review and audit of the choices available and made (as described in Chapter 14 of this book) should be completed by a knowledgeable committee of internal and external auditors annually, and a summary of the current or recommended security implementation should be presented to executive management annually as well. This process need not be expensive nor time consuming, but the benefit will be measurable as new attacks appear and new technologies surface.

Finally, technology must not become a smokescreen for what is happening within the core of a security product. Security is an essential element of an information technology environment, and as such, must be chosen with care. A deep understanding of the processes might require some additional education in a specific field (such as optics, electronics, or even introductory quantum theory), but the benefit of such an understanding is that no marketing material will succeed in obscuring the true limitations and capabilities of a technology from someone who has taken time to master its basic principles. To quote Francis Bacon, "knowledge is power."

Roger R. Dube
Rochester, NY

# INTRODUCTION

Since ancient times, mankind has had a need to communicate with complete privacy and authenticity. Signatures, trusted couriers, secret passwords, and sealing wax were all elements of early systems that sought to authenticate or otherwise protect messages between two parties. As wars between nations became fiercer, the need for secure communication increased. Over time we have witnessed the development of increasingly complex ciphers, cryptography, and even the introduction of the Enigma machine.

With the advent of electronic computers, there has been an explosion of activity in the creation of new cryptographic algorithms. Many of these systems required the use of random numbers in some aspect of their operation, but John von Neumann, who is regarded as the father of computer science, strongly cautioned people against the use of any form of software algorithm to generate random numbers (see Chapter 1, page 12 of this book). Von Neumann recognized that only a physical process can produce a truly random, unpredictable number. The output of a mathematical algorithm, by its very nature, can be predicted if the algorithm is returned to the initial condition of a previous time. Moreover, as explained in Chapter 3, there are fundamental concerns with the distribution or sharing of keys. Against this setting, the exponential growth of processing power has enhanced the ability of hackers to break algorithms and keys. So how do we move security forward?

Hardware devices can tie a computer system and its user to the physical world. Proper protection of such devices against tampering can further strengthen the system. The use of person-specific information that can only be obtained in person (such as biometrics) can add credibility to the authentication process. New technologies that employ location-specific signatures can be used to place such an authenticated person at an authenticated location, provided that the technology cannot be spoofed or defeated.

With this backdrop in mind, this book presents computer security from the perspective of employing hardware-based security technologies to construct systems that cannot be broken by hackers. Armed with a review of basic computer security concepts and analysis techniques, the book quickly moves into the realm of hardware-based security technologies. Such technologies span a wide range of topics, including physics-based random number generators, biometric devices, trusted computing systems, location awareness, and quantum cryptography.

Each of these technologies is examined with an eye toward possible attack avenues. By following the types of approaches currently being employed by hackers to defeat hardware-based security devices, the reader should develop an understanding of the means by which security technologies can be evaluated for possible use in any given security system. With an understanding of the security goals of a system, any technology device can be analyzed for possible vulnerabilities if used in that system.

# Chapter 1

## THE ELEMENTS OF COMPUTER SECURITY

Recent statistics on computer security breaches demonstrate that there has been an explosive growth of successful computer attacks worldwide. Valuable personal and corporate information is being compromised, and computer systems that control communications and critical infrastructure operations are being attacked. The continued success of these attacks demands answers to questions such as: What is the root cause of the problem? And what steps can be taken to prevent successful attacks?

In order to address these questions in a systematic fashion, it is important to review the basic components that form the foundation of current computer security. Since the roles and interplay of these components are often central to attacks that capitalize on weaknesses of a security system, a clear understanding of these components is a necessary prerequisite for mounting a solid defense.

This chapter presents an introduction to the primary elements of computer security. The terminology and fundamental principles behind each element are discussed, and, where appropriate, limitations and attack

1

avenues are presented. The chapter is intended to act as a primary reference and overview for the rest of the book.

## CRYPTOGRAPHY

The first element that comes to mind when a person thinks about computer security is cryptography. Cryptography is the process of converting an information-bearing message to something that appears to be completely unintelligible "gibberish," or performing the inverse process (decoding a cryptographically protected message). These processes are referred to as encryption and decryption, respectively.

There are two basic forms of cryptographic processes—symmetric, in which the same key is used to encrypt and decrypt a message, and asymmetric, in which the key employed to encrypt a message is different from the key employed to decrypt the message.

A cryptographic encryption process consists of an algorithm, such as the data encryption standard three times (triple DES), advanced encryption standard (AES) or a host of others, that takes an input string of characters or numbers (the information we wish to protect) and converts the string to "gibberish." In order to do so, it must be set to a predictable initial state, and it requires an encryption key. As explained above, in symmetric key cryptography the same key is used to encrypt and decrypt a file. Asymmetric cryptography uses different keys for encryption and decryption and so employs a more complex algorithm. This difference gives symmetric key cryptography an advantage of faster processing and therefore less computing overhead. There are issues with symmetric key cryptography, however.

### Symmetric Key Cryptography

The first fundamental issue with symmetric key cryptography is the process by which the key is transmitted securely between parties that wish to employ the process. Clearly the key cannot be transmitted between the parties without any form of protection—its interception by the simplest packet sniffer would effectively yield the key to a listening party that then would have full knowledge of any subsequent communications. Encrypting the key in order to send it also requires that this second key be shared between the two parties. The requirements for transmission of keys layer upon one another ad infinitum. This simply won't work.

The key could be sent by trusted courier. This might work for communication between countries or in situations where the stakes are very high (situations involving decoding of missile launch codes or military plans), but in the world of everyday computing the concept of using trusted couriers to hand-deliver specific encryption keys to every possible participant in an encrypted communication is not practical.

A second fundamental issue with symmetric key cryptography is that a different key is needed for each potential participant. The delivery of keys aside, the management of systems where each recipient has a different key rapidly becomes an exponentially more difficult task as the number of recipients grows. Key management ultimately limits the value of symmetric key cryptography.

### Asymmetric Key Cryptography

The issues with symmetric key cryptography were solved in part when, in 1976, a revolutionary paper was published by Whitfield Diffie and Martin Hellman of Stanford University[1]. In this paper, Diffie and Hellman first described "public key cryptography" (also referred to as asymmetric key cryptography or the Diffie-Hellman algorithm). In asymmetric key cryptography, complementary keys are employed: one key is used for encryption and a second key is used for decryption. Moreover, the encryption process is target-specific—that is, one encrypts a file in a manner that only the intended recipient will hold the second key for decryption. In short, the method revealed by Diffie and Hellman removed the need for transmission of a secret key as required in symmetric key cryptography.

It is important to understand the revolutionary manner in which asymmetric key cryptography works, since its operation has become fundamental to much of today's cryptographic systems and has bearing on issues related to hacking.

The Diffie-Hellman algorithm employs a symmetry property in mathematics. That symmetry is:

(Equation 1) $$x^{(a)b} = x^{(b)a}$$

That is, a number x raised to the power a is then raised to the power b. The result is identical to the number x raised to the power b, which is then raised to the power a. As an example, let consider the case where $x = 7$, a $= 2$, and $b = 3$. First calculate $x^{(a)}$ and $x^{(b)}$:

(Equation 2) $\qquad x^{(a)} = 7^{(2)} = 49$

(Equation 3) $\qquad x^{(b)} = 7^{(3)} = 343$

Then raising the results of Equation 2 above to the power b=3, we find:

(Equation 4) $\qquad x^{(a)b} = 49^3 = 117,649$

Similarly, raising the results of Equation 3 to the power a=2 yields:

(Equation 5) $\qquad x^{(b)a} = 343^2 = 117,649$

This mathematical symmetry, combined with one additional process, establishes the core of asymmetric key cryptography. By further modifying the result of the above symmetric process with a modulo function employing a prime number in which the result of the intermediate exponentiation (Equations 2 and 3 above) is divided by a prime number and replaced with the remainder of the division, the process assumes a quality that makes it mathematically nearly impossible to reverse. So the modified equations become:

(Equation 6) $\qquad x^{(a)} \bmod p$

(Equation 7) $\qquad x^{(b)} \bmod p$

Imagine that two parties wish to establish an encrypted communication using symmetric key cryptography, but want to avoid the transmission of a secret key due to the fundamental problems cited above. For the purposes of illustration, consider the simple case where the key (or "password") to be used with symmetric key cryptography will consist of a number (the extension of the concept to complex passwords or pass phrases is straightforward and will not be discussed here). Using the cryptographic convention, the two parties will be Alice and Bob. Alice and Bob agree in advance to use $p = 11$ and a base $x = 7$. Alice chooses her "secret key" (known only to her and never transmitted or shared) $a = 2$. Using Equation 6 above, Alice computes $x^{(a)} \bmod p$ and sends the result (5) unencrypted to Bob. This is effectively her "Public Key":

(Equation 8) $\qquad$ Alice's public key $K_A = x^{(a)} \bmod$ $p = 7^{(2)} \bmod 11 = 5$

Alice transmits her public key in the clear to Bob. Bob, in turn, chooses his own "secret key" b = 3. Using Equation 7 above, Bob computes $x^{(b)}$ mod p (his public key) and sends the result to Alice:

(Equation 9)  Bob's public key = $K_B = x^{(b)}$ mod p = $7^{(3)}$ mod 11 = 2

Alice can now compute the key to be used to communicate with Bob. She uses Bob's public key in conjunction with her own secret key to determine the shared key:

(Equation 10)  shared key = $K_B^{(a)}$ mod 11 = $2^2$ mod 11 = 4 mod 11 = 4

Bob, armed with Alice's public key, uses his own secret key to determine the shared key:

(Equation 11)  shared key = $K_A^{(b)}$ mod 11 = $5^3$ mod 11 = 125 mod 11 = 4

Both Alice and Bob now know the shared key to be used in any subsequent encrypted transmissions using symmetric cryptography with the shared key to encrypt or decrypt the messages. The beauty of asymmetric key cryptography is that Bob and Alice were able to compute a shared key specific to their encrypted intercommunications without having to transmit the shared key at any time. Rather, this asymmetric cryptography involved the sharing of two public keys, which then enabled each of the two parties to determine the shared key to be used for their particular communication. It is left as an exercise to the reader to show that the shared key to be used by Alice with a third party that has a different secret key (and therefore a different public key) will employ a different shared key.

In practice, the prime number p should be at least 300 digits long, and the secret keys "a" and "b" should be at least 100 digits long. With these constraints on a, b, and p, it has been estimated that all of mankind's computing power will not be able to find the secret key "a" given only x, p, and $x^a$ mod p. Note also that x need not be large—the use of 2 or 5 is common.

## PASSWORDS AND KEYS

A cryptographic key can be comprised of a password. Passwords have been used since ancient times to control access to resources, identify a person as an insider, or identify an unknown soldier as friend or foe. In computer security, a password is a secret that should, in principle, be known only to the creator of the password. In this capacity it is referred to as "something you know." As long as the password is sufficiently difficult to guess and has not been written down anywhere, it can have some value in the protection of information when combined with cryptography. A password is usually employed as part (or all) of a cryptographic key.

In spite of its name, a "password" need not be a word or phrase at all. It may be a string of numbers (a PIN or passcode) or a mixture of letters, numbers, and special characters (such as $#&*@!). In fact, the more obscure a string of characters, numbers, and symbols, the more difficult it will be for an attacker to guess the password. But, just as complex passwords may be difficult to guess, they may be difficult for the owner to remember. The tradeoff between the desirability of "complexity" and the undesirability of "difficulty to memorize" often leads users to one or more of the following actions:

- The length of the password is minimized
- The password is written down
- The complex password uses a substitution mechanism that is easy to remember (for example, the password "strong" might become "$tr0ng")

### Password/Key Strength

In general, strong authentication techniques require that a person prove ownership of a hard-to-guess secret to the target computer. In a shared-secret system, a user would transmit the password during the login operation, and the computer would verify that the password matched its internal records. More sophisticated systems employ an additional encryption or hashing step to avoid vulnerabilities due to eavesdropping of the communication link.

An important measure of the strength of a password is to determine the *average attack space*. In this measurement, a mathematical estimate is made of the average number of guesses an attacker would have to make in order to guess the correct password. As an example, consider a bicycle lock comprised of four rotating cylinders, each with 10 possible positions (numbers). Since each cylinder adds a multiplicative factor of 10 to the number possible combinations that must be tried, a five-cylinder lock is ten times more difficult to guess than a four-cylinder lock. The average attack space does not include any time estimate required to guess a password. It is best to avoid time in the comparison of password strengths since, in the computer field, processing speed increases each year, so the time required to break a password gets smaller each year. The time factor can be introduced later, after password strengths have been compared based on their average attack space.

If all possible values of a password are equally likely to occur, then on average an attacker will find the right password after trying half of those possible values. Thus, an average attack space reflects the need to search half of the possible combinations, not all of them.

In practice, password choices have bias which further reduces number of trials before guessing the correct password. The average attack space should reflect any bias that might be present when the password was created. In the case of a four-digit bicycle lock, dates are relatively easy for people to remember and are often expressed as four digits, so the attack space is likely reduced to reflect possible dates rather than all 10000 combinations.

Password biases give power to "dictionary attacks." Letter-based passwords are most likely to employ words that the creator can easily remember. Armed with a modest amount of information about the characteristic of the password (such as a hashed version of the password that may have been intercepted during a transmission or retrieved from a database on the target computer) a brute force dictionary attack can proceed through common words in the dictionary and common password hashing algorithms until a match is found. Once found, the password has been "guessed" and the system is now cracked.

Since most trial-and-error attacks are directed against cryptographic systems, and since computer systems measure everything as powers of 2 (representing the fundamental binary nature of bitwise computing), it is convenient to represent average attack spaces in powers of two. If, for example, a dictionary attack finds a password after trying 16,384 words, then the average attack space is:

$$16384 = 2^{14}$$

As a calibration of the "difficulty" of an attack space of $2^{14}$, it is noteworthy that a successful attack on the Data Encryption Standard (DES) by a special purpose computer called Deep Crack[2] involved $2^{54}$ attempts, on average, to attack its 56-bit key. An attack space of $2^{40}$, for example, is relatively easy to crack.

In 2005, a team of researchers at Cambridge University[3] performed a study of password usage. Of the passwords used by the control group in the experiments that sought to create stronger passwords, 35 percent of their passwords were cracked. The general population uses passwords that are relatively easy to guess.

### Password/Key Storage and Theft

In a theft attack, a program of some sort is usually installed on a target computer without the knowledge of the user. The installation is usually accomplished by a "Trojan" program that appears to be innocent but whose actual task is to install the theft attack program. The theft attack program is usually designed to produce a window that resembles a login prompt or otherwise invites the user to reveal a password. Users will then type their passwords into this program, where the password is saved or forwarded to the attacker for later use. A similar attack program called "phishing" has been developed and is propagated by emails that appear legitimate. These programs usually request that the user confirm his account information (including entering his password) or the account will be closed. The user's secret information is then forwarded to the attacker. A related attack is *spearphishing* in which a specific user or organization is targeted by the phishing attack in order to obtain specific information.

Anti-virus and anti-spyware programs can sometimes detect and delete such attack programs. But ultimately the user needs a means to determine whether or not any window being displayed can be trusted. If each parent in the chain of windows that spawned a password window can be trusted, then the login prompt window must be trusted and it is safe to enter a password. This concept is called a *trusted path*.

One implementation of a trusted path involves the activation of the trusted path through a particular key sequence, such as Ctl-Alt-Del in Windows. The keyboard driver captures the sequence and always transfers control to some trusted software that then displays a password login window.

The unspoken requirement in this logic is that the keyboard driver itself must be trusted. That, in turn, means that the operating system running the keyboard driver must be trusted so that bogus keyboard drivers cannot be substituted. The OS image that was used to boot up the system may have been altered. In fact, even the boot loader might have been altered to read from a compromised location on the disk. The demands placed on the chain of trust become progressively more complex. If a complete chain of trust can be created from the initial hardware layer down through the password window, the technique of the trusted path offers a defense against password theft.

## Passwords and Authentication

Passwords are not only used for encryption purposes. They also can play a role in authenticating the user. Authentication sometimes involves the prior sharing of one or more "secrets" and then the subsequent checking of the secrets being presented by a user against what has previously been shared.

The process of authenticating a person is different than that of authenticating a computer, because a person is not comprised of numerical information that is relatively easy to access, as is true for a computer. Authentication of a person requires the capture of numerical information through the use of a device (a fingerprint, a voice print, an image, a password entered on a keyboard, etc.) that, with some high degree of confidence, should be unique to the intended person. Authentication may contain one or more "factors" that are evaluated by the receiving party in determining whether or not a person is in fact who he claims to be. These factors may include:

- Something that the user knows (a secret not possibly known by anyone else)
- Something that the user has (something unique in his possession)
- Something that the user "is" (such as a fingerprint)

### *Something You Know*
In authentication, passwords fall into the category of "something the user knows." Passwords can be stolen or shared by unwitting users. So the authentication of remote users needs additional components that make spoofing difficult. Perhaps authentication should require that the user not only know the password, but also have in his possession some unique piece of hardware, "something you have."

### *Something You Have*
The additional requirement for a piece of hardware creates *two-factor authentication* in which "something you know" must be accompanied by "something you have." Various tokens and smart-card technologies often provide this second authentication factor. Neither factor alone is as strong as the combination. A password alone can be cracked, stolen, or learned, enabling an attacker to masquerade as the legitimate user. A token alone can be stolen, once again allowing an attacker to spoof an identity. Two-factor authentication, however, now requires that the attacker overcome both hurdles.

There are many examples of hardware devices that are used in two-factor authentication, and these will be discussed more deeply in subsequent chapters of this book. They include:

- A magnetic strip card, such as an ID or credit card.
- Proximity card or radio frequency identification ("RFID"). These cards transmit stored information to a monitor via radio frequency electronics embedded within the card.
- Challenge/response cards and cryptographic calculators. These are usually smart cards and perform some sort of cryptographic calculation.

Why stop at two-factor authentication? By adding something that is person-specific and is measured, a third authentication factor (or perhaps a replacement of one of the two preceding authentication factors) can add an additional hurdle that significantly raises the difficulty of successful attacks.

### Something You Are

Humans, like animals, recognize others by evaluating a variety of stimuli and comparing them to stored knowledge about others they have met. Facial features (hair color, eye color, smile), body size and shape, mannerisms, sound, perhaps even smell might all contribute to the total set of characteristics that are subconsciously employed in the recognition of others. Collectively, we refer to this as "something you are." The degree to which we can find unique characteristics that can be measured and used to uniquely separate people from one another (fingerprint readers, for example) determines whether or not such a measurement can be employed in authentication. These personal characteristics must be:

- Easily measured
- Accurate and stable over long periods of time
- Unique, with very low likelihood of false positives and false negatives
- Difficult to spoof or predict

Devices that accomplish this are called *biometrics*, and examples include:

- Retinal scan
- Fingerprint reader
- Handprint reader
- Voice print

- Keystroke timing
- Signature

In order to be able to use a biometric technology to recognize and authenticate a person, his biometric characteristics must be stable over a long period of time, and they must be stored in some concise digital form for future use. Fingerprint readers, for example, do not store entire images of a person's fingerprint. Rather, specific inflection points and other stable features within the fingerprint are measured and recorded for later comparison to presented data.

This raises two immediate concerns. First, the biometric characteristic must be stable in order to be recognizable—it doesn't change. This means that there is an average attack space for this fixed characteristic, and it, like any other password, may ultimately be guessed. Second, the fact that the characteristic has been stored means that there is a file or database somewhere that an attacker could steal in order to break the system and spoof the target's identity. Biometric devices are very convenient and purported to be unique, but we should not rely entirely on this uniqueness as being an ultimate solution to authentication of passwords. Fingerprint readers and the analytical techniques that support them normally have error rates of 5 percent and more. Biometric devices will be explored in more detail in subsequent chapters of this book.

So humans are not the best sources of passwords or other unique, unpredictable strings that can be used for encryption keys or authentication. An alternate approach that attempts to solve this predictability uses random number generators to create progressively more complex keys with large average attack spaces.


## RANDOM-NUMBER GENERATORS

Aside from the generation of keys on an as-needed basis by asking a user to enter a password, the creation of cryptographic keys can also be accomplished through the use of random-number generators. A random-number generator returns a random number on request. A good random-number generator should have several characteristics in order to satisfy strict mathematical requirements of "randomness." It should:

- Produce numbers that pass major known criteria for "randomness"
- Have no repetitive pattern in its output

- Have no initial conditions that reset the output to repeat a sequence
- Not be spoofable
- Not be susceptible to commandeering, in which the generator is forced to produce a predictable stream

There are two basic types of random-number generators: pseudo-random-number generators (PRGs) and hardware-based random-number generators.

**Pseudo-Random-Number Generators (PRGs)**

PRGs are algorithms that, upon request, return a number spanning some range of values. Because they are software-based, delivery of the PRG to remote locations is easily accomplished by email, ftp, or other electronic distribution techniques. There are many PRGs in existence, and the degree to which they provide a sequence of numbers that have no discernable pattern is an important figure of merit that should be considered when choosing a PRG. The techniques used to determine the degree of randomness produced by any source of random numbers is beyond the scope of this book. However, PRGs are algorithms, and as such, they can be placed in a predictable state. That state might be set by introducing a "seed" number into the algorithm. The seed sets the initial conditions from which the PRG proceeds to generate its output. The troubling fact is that, if a PRG is set to an initial condition and the sequence of numbers generated are recorded, when set to the same initial conditions the PRG will produce exactly the same sequence of numbers. These properties led John von Neumann, considered by some to be the father of modern computer science, to say the following: "Any one who considers arithmetical methods of producing random digits is, of course, in a state of sin."[4]

**Hardware-Based Random-Number Generators**

A powerful alternative to the PRG is a hardware-based random-number generator. This is a device residing on a local machine or a stand-alone unit that includes electronics that produce random numbers. There are several types of hardware-based random-number generators that will be discussed in more detail in subsequent chapters of this book.

In measurement of a user's interaction with the computer:

- The user moves the mouse randomly until a sufficiently long key has been built

- The user measures the time interval between typing of letters on the keyboard to produce random numbers that can be used to build a key

Noisy diodes/thermal noise/field-programmable gate array ("FPGA") devices:

- Ring oscillators that amplify thermal noise[5]

In devices that use radioactive decay times:

- a minuscule piece of radioactive material emits particles as it decays. The time interval between successive decays is random.

Radio-frequency ("RF") noise:

- If properly executed to avoid potential susceptibility to commandeering through overwhelming transmitters, the RF can provide several sources of high quality noise.

### Hybrid Hardware/Software Random-Number Generators

An approach to stronger key generation using pseudo-random number generators is to use a hybrid of PRGs and hardware. A PRG that is encased in a smart card, for example, could be protected in a way that prevents external access to its operation, including setting of seed conditions, which is one of the paths for commandeering a PRG. It could be argued that a hardware-encased PRG loses the portability advantages of a software-only approach to key generation. But the hybrid approach offers an advantage over software-only solutions when combined with key storage, as discussed below. Tradeoffs need to be considered in evaluating these approaches.

### *Key Generation*
The creation of 100-digit secret keys can be accomplished in several ways. Due to the pivotal role that secret keys play in asymmetric key cryptography, it is important (some might argue "essential") that they have the following properties:

- If created by the user, the key should be difficult to guess—the use of common words should be avoided to prevent vulnerability to dictionary attacks.

- If the key is generated automatically (this is possible since it is generally a one-time process), it must be created using a random number generator that has the characteristics of randomness cited above.

Key generators must pass at least two "tests" when being evaluated for possible use in cryptography:

- Test 1: Does the output have any discernable pattern?
- Test 2: Can the generator be forced to reproduce its output by resetting initial conditions or through the introduction of external manipulation?

These tests will be applied to the random-number generators in the chapters that follow. A key generator that fails either test could potentially be used to subvert a security system.

Hardware-based key generators avoid the weaknesses common to PRGs cited above. For this and other reasons that will become clear in subsequent chapters of this book, hardware-based computer security implementations and technologies offer enhanced strength over their software-only counterparts.

## SECURITY AND THE INTERNET

The Internet employs several communication protocols to achieve its functionality. The two most important Internet protocols are transmission control protocol (TCP) and the Internet protocol (IP)—collectively referred to as TCP/IP. Developed in the early 1980s, the specifications for these important protocols were finalized during a period when their use was dominated by small groups of users who (appropriately) trusted each other. As a consequence, security was not built into the specification. As a result, today's Internet lacks even the most basic mechanisms for security, such as authentication or encryption. These have been added as an afterthought, and the fact that these features are not built in is becoming increasingly problematic.

The IP portion of TCP/IP is the network layer of the Internet. Its job is to route and send a packet of data to its destination. The data packets travel through a sequence of routers before they reach their goal. At each intermediate point in this transmission, nodes determine the next hop for the data packet. This provides the strength of dynamic routing—in the event that a portion of the network goes down for any reason (such as power failures), a data packet would be rerouted through a different path. It is very possible that two data packets from the same source might take entirely different paths to get to their destination, much like two cars leaving a neighborhood might take entirely different streets to get to the same grocery store due to traffic jams.

This dynamic quality introduces a degree of unpredictability in arrival times of data packets. In the same way that there is no guarantee that two data packets will arrive at their destination following the same path, there is also no guarantee that they will arrive in sequence. IP is a "best efforts" system that does not assure that packets will arrive or in what sequence. The task of reassembling all the data packets is left to higher layers in the protocol stack. Moreover, the data packet and its header (the "address" that contains the destination and route information for the data packet) are not encrypted—it is a simple matter to replace the intended address of a data packet with an alternate that delivers the data packets to an attacker. The IP protocol will oblige.

The "higher layer" that has the responsibility of data-packet management referred to above is the TCP layer. In today's Internet, the TCP layer provides the guaranteed delivery and also is responsible for correctly reassembling the file from all of its composite data packets. It communicates with the sender and receiver through various handshakes and timing mechanisms that trigger repeated requests. The handshakes that the TCP protocol employs are called SYN and ACK—when computer A seeks a connection with computer B, computer A sends a SYN flag to B. Upon receiving the SYN flag, computer B responds with an ACK flag. This is the basic connection handshake that initiates a connection.

One of the basic attacks that can be performed on the Internet is the SYN flood. In this attack, a malicious programmer arranges for his computer to send a very rapid series of SYN requests to a target computer. If the target computer obliges and returns an ACK for each SYN flag and does not "recognize" the flood as being malicious ("normal" computers don't behave this way), it will quickly consume all available ports and processing power trying to satisfy the SYN flood. This is one way to create what is referred to as a "denial of service" in which the target computer effectively cannot respond to any other requests.

Simultaneous SYN packets from two different (attacking) computers can cause confusion at the target machine and cause a connection port to freeze, creating an opportunity for malicious attackers to capitalize on other weaknesses in the TCP/IP protocol in order to gain access to information on the target machine.

As mentioned above, the IP layer does no form of authentication to determine if the IP address of a data packet actually originated at that IP address. Another form of attack, called IP spoofing, replaces an attacking computer's actual IP address in the TCP/IP data packet headers with the IP address of another computer, spoofing its IP address. Since there is no authentication of the IP address, the target computer sends its responses to the spoofed IP address, rather than the IP address of the attacker. There is no record of any unusual SYN request activity from the attacker's IP address, but rather the SYN activity is seen as coming from the spoofed IP address. The attacker remains anonymous. Any attempt by the IT department that owns the targeted computer to contact the ISP of the "attacker" in order to shut down the account results in an unsubstantiated claim in one case (there was no SYN flood originating on the computer whose IP address was spoofed) or the suspension of an innocent third party in another case. Such an IP spoofing attack can be used to establish a one-way communication with a target computer, and techniques can be applied to convert this to a two-way communication in which the attacker can take control of the target computer or otherwise gain access to protected information. Additional IP spoofing attacks and other ways to take advantage of the weaknesses in today's Internet will be discussed in a subsequent chapter.

Hackers have been able to capitalize on the host of vulnerabilities that the lack of encryption and authentication has created in today's Internet. The use of methods that employ the strengths of hardware-based (as opposed to software-based) security technologies is the central focus of this book.

## REFERENCES

[1] W. Diffie and M.E.Hellman, "New directions in cryptography," *IEEE Trans. Inform. Theory*, IT-22, 6, 1976, pp. 644–654.

[2] *Cracking DES: Secrets of Encryption Research, Wiretap Politics, and Chip Design*, by the Electronic Frontier Foundation (Sebastopol, CA: O'Reilly & Associates, 1998).

[3] "The Memorability and Security of Passwords," Yan, J., Blackwell, A., Anderson, R., Grant, A., in *Security and Usability*, edited by Cranor, L.F., Garfinkel, S., 2005, p. 129.

[4] Quoted in *The Art of Computer Programming*, Donald Knuth, Vol II (2nd Edition).

[5] "A High-Speed Oscillator-Based Truly Random Number Source for Cryptographic Applications on a Smart Card IC" Bucci, Luzzi, Trifiletti and Varanonuovo, *IEEE Transactions on Computers*, April 2003, Vol 52, No. 4, pp. 403–409.

# Chapter 2

## CRYPTOGRAPHY APPROACHES AND ATTACKS

Encryption's central role in computer security demands a thorough understanding by IT professionals who wish to employ it. The IT professional needs a firm command of cryptography in order to build proper defenses against breaches and attacks. This chapter presents a more in-depth review of cryptographic techniques and their potential weaknesses. Knowledge of basic cryptographic approaches, combined with an understanding of the generation and distribution of keys discussed in Chapter 3, will provide the foundation required to examine the robustness of hardware-based computer-security technologies discussed in subsequent chapters.

### SYMMETRIC KEY CRYPTOGRAPHY

As explained in Chapter 1, symmetric key cryptography uses the same key to encrypt and decrypt a file. There are many symmetric key algorithms that have been developed over the years, including (but by no means limited to):

- One-time pads
- DES and Triple DES
- International Data-Encryption Algorithm (IDEA)
- Rivest Cipher 4 (RC4)
- Blowfish
- AES
- Quantum cryptography

Before examining specific cryptographic algorithms in detail, it is important to separate such ciphers into two categories: block and stream ciphers. A block cipher is a symmetric key cryptographic process that operates on fixed-length groups of bits called "blocks" using the same transformation for each block. During encryption, a block cipher might take a fixed-length block of 128 bits from plain text, for example, and, using a secret key, create a 128-bit block of cipher text. Decryption reverses the process. In contrast, a stream cipher operates on individual bits at a time, so the transformation changes depending on the content.

**One-Time Pad**

A one-time pad (a variation of the Vernam cipher) employs a string of random letters or numbers that is at least as long as the target message to be encrypted. Both the sender and the receiver must have identical copies of the pad, and each string is used only once (hence the term "one-time"—in its original form, the random string was written on two identical pads of paper, and the top sheet destroyed after use).

In operation, the message to be encrypted is merged with the string of random letters or numbers using an exclusive-OR process (XOR) that combines a bit from the input (the plain-text file) and a corresponding bit from the key stream to produce the encrypted output bit using the rules in Table 2.1.

The recipient decrypts the message by using his copy of the one-time pad and reversing the above process. Since each sequence is used only once, intruders can't crack the code by analyzing many encrypted messages.

In practice, one-time pads are difficult to use since both the sender and the receiver must have identical copies. This distribution issue, combined with the requirement that the pad be as long as the target message, often makes it impractical.

**Table 2.1**    The XOR process.

| input bit | stream bit | output bit |
|-----------|------------|------------|
| 0         | 0          | 0          |
| 1         | 0          | 1          |
| 0         | 1          | 0          |
| 1         | 1          | 0          |

**DES and Triple DES**

In 1972, the U.S. National Bureau of Standards, or NBS (now called the National Institute of Standards and Technology, or NIST), determined that a strong cryptographic algorithm was needed to protect nonclassified information. The algorithm needed to be inexpensive, widely available, and very secure. NBS envisioned something that would be available to the general public and that could be used in a wide variety of applications. NBS asked for public proposals for such an algorithm. In 1974 IBM submitted the Lucifer algorithm, which appeared to meet most of NBS's design requirements.

After evaluation by the National Security Agency, the modified Lucifer algorithm was adopted by NBS as a federal standard. In 1977, NBS published the data encryption standard[1] (DES). DES subsequently became an ANSI standard[2]. This symmetric cryptographic algorithm uses a 56-bit (7-byte) key and maps a 64-bit input block of plain text onto a 64-bit output block of encrypted text. This bit size is considered a rather small key for today's computing power, and, as a result, this algorithm has become very controversial.

The core process of DES encryption involves permutations of bits. The entire DES process is lengthy and beyond the scope or focus of this book; nonetheless, it is instructive to gain at least a surface understanding of the process. The process begins with a 64-bit (8-byte) key. The least significant bit of each byte is a parity bit, which is set to 0 or 1 so that the total number of bits in each byte is odd. The parity bits of the 8 bytes comprising the DES key are ignored, leaving a total active key length of 56 bits.

The first step is to pass the 64-bit key through a permutation called permuted choice 1 (PC-1). The PC-1 table is given in Table 2.2. Rather than proceed through a complete example of the process, let us consider how a single bit passes through the permutation. Extension to all the bits is straightforward from this process.

Consider how bit 35 of the original 64-bit key is moved to a new location. Observe in PC-1 below that the number 35 appears in column 5 and is in the row labeled 15. Add the row and column in which the bit appears to obtain the new bit position: $5 + 15 = 20$.

So bit 35 of the original key is placed in bit 20 of the new key. Bits that correspond to the parity bits have been excluded from the PC-1 table. These unused parity bits from the original key are discarded.

The new key is now used to create 16 48-bit subkeys. The process for creating the subkeys begins by breaking the newly created 56-bit key into two 28-bit halves, a left-hand half (LH) and a right-hand half (RH).

Next, the round number R is set to 1 (16 rounds are ultimately needed). Now rotate the bits in the left-hand half, LH, left by the number of bits below the number $R=1$ in Table 2.3. Rotate the RH half left by the same number of bits.

**Table 2.2**  PC-1: Permuted Choice 1.

| Bit | 0 | 1 | 2 | 3 | 4 | 5 | 6 |
|-----|-----|-----|-----|-----|-----|-----|-----|
| 1   | 57  | 49  | 41  | 33  | 25  | 17  | 9   |
| 8   | 1   | 58  | 50  | 42  | 34  | 26  | 18  |
| 15  | 10  | 2   | 59  | 51  | 43  | 35  | 27  |
| 22  | 19  | 11  | 3   | 60  | 52  | 44  | 36  |
| 29  | 63  | 55  | 47  | 39  | 31  | 23  | 15  |
| 36  | 7   | 62  | 54  | 46  | 38  | 30  | 22  |
| 43  | 14  | 6   | 61  | 53  | 45  | 37  | 29  |
| 50  | 21  | 13  | 5   | 28  | 20  | 12  | 4   |

**Table 2.3**  Subkey rotation table.

| Round Number | 1 | 2 | 3 | 4 | 5 | 6 | 7 | 8 | 9 | 10 | 11 | 12 | 13 | 14 | 15 | 16 |
|-----|---|---|---|---|---|---|---|---|---|----|----|----|----|----|----|----|
| Number of bits to rotate | 1 | 1 | 2 | 2 | 2 | 2 | 2 | 2 | 1 | 2 | 2 | 2 | 2 | 2 | 2 | 1 |

Join the LH and RH together (after rotation) to get a new K. Finally, use a second permutation table, PC-2, to convert the new K to a final subkey, K(R). (PC-2 is not reproduced here for brevity.)

Finally, two additional permutation tables will be employed to encrypt and decrypt the plain text that one seeks to protect. These tables, called IP (initial permutation) and IP-1 (inverse initial permutation), are used in much the same manner as PC-1 above. Examination of the IP and IP$^{-1}$ (available on multiple websites) will show that the two tables are inverses of one another. Passing a plain-text 64-bit input through IP, then passing the result through IP$^{-1}$, will yield the original plain text.

To summarize the remaining process, DES encryption involves a complex series of steps. The 64-bit input is first permuted using the IP table. The output is then subjected to sixteen rounds, each of which takes the 64-bit output of the previous round and a 48-bit per-round key and produces a 64-bit output. After the final round, the 64-bit output is subjected to inverse initial permutation. DES decryption is essentially done by running this process backwards.

A flow chart of the DES encryption process summarizes the primary aspects of this algorithm in Figure 2.1.

The result of the DES is encrypted text in which there is no one-to-one mapping of input character to encrypted character—the letter "e" in the plain-text file does not always produced a "y" in the encrypted text. In simpler symmetric cryptographic algorithms, a one-to-one map would be produced, thereby greatly increasing the chance of cracking.

Nonetheless, 56 bits is considered a small (weak) key size in the face of today's progressively more powerful computers. This is true because a brute force attack (in which a program simply proceeds to try all possible guesses for the key) is well within reach when facing a 56-bit key. Let us examine the difficulty of guessing a 56-bit key using today's computers. Each bit of a 56-bit key can have one of two values—either a zero or a one—so the total number of possible combinations of these bits that comprise a 56-bit key is:

$$\text{Number of 56-bit combinations} = 2^{56}$$

Assume that a carefully designed personal computer program today can perform $10^9$ 56-bit guesses per second. Since there are 3600 seconds per hour, 24 hours per day, and 365.25 days per year, the amount of time it would take a PC to guess a 56-bit key would be about:

$$\text{Time to guess} = 2^{56}/(10^9 \times 3600 \times 24 \times 365.25) = 2.28 \text{ years per PC}$$

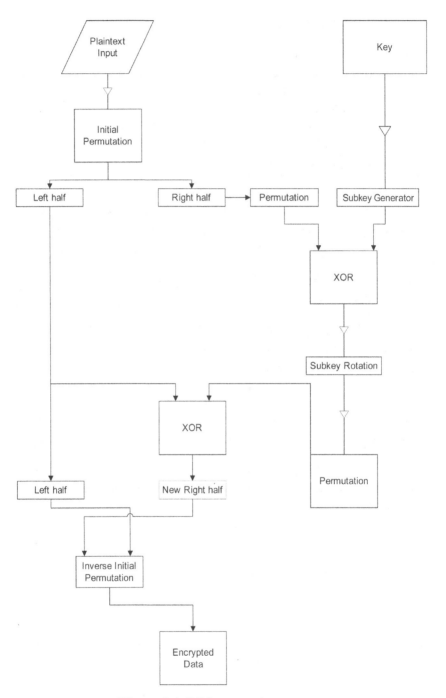

**Figure 2.1** DES encryption process.

Clearly, a few computers dedicated to the task of guessing and limited to orthogonal guessing spaces (to avoid duplication) could collectively guess the 56-bit key in relatively short order.

As a result of this concern, the key size was increased to 168 bits (three 56-bit keys) in triple DES. The triple DES algorithm employs these three 56-bit keys in sequence, as captured in the flow chart in Figure 2.2.

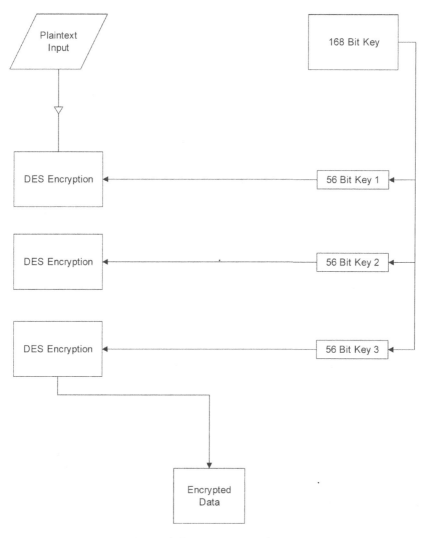

**Figure 2.2** Triple DES encryption process.

Triple DES gained popularity for a period of time until NIST replaced the DES encryption standard with the more recent advanced encryption standard (AES), which employs a key size of up to 256 bits. A calculation of the time required to guess a 256-bit key (using the brute force method shown above) yields a time of:

$$\text{Time to guess} = 2^{256}/(10^9 \times 3600 \times 24 \times 365.25) =$$
$$3.67 \times 10^{60} \text{ years per PC}$$

This is significantly longer than the time required to guess a 56-bit key! AES is discussed in more detail later in this chapter.

### International Data-Encryption Algorithm

The international data-encryption algorithm (IDEA) was developed in 1991 at ETH Zurich, which is also referred to as the Swiss Federal Institute of Technology. It is a block cipher that uses a 128-bit key to encrypt a 64-bit block of plain text into a 64-bit block of cipher text.

IDEA's general algorithm (also a symmetric cryptographic algorithm) is very similar to DES. It creates per-round keys from the 128-bit key and then performs 17 rounds, each round taking 64 bits of input to produce a 64-bit output. The details of each round's operation are more complicated than those used in DES and will not be reproduced here, but they also involve an irreversible process of permutations of bits using both the input and per-round keys.

IDEA offers both a performance advantage over DES as well as employing a much bigger key size, which translates into greater security.

### Rivest Cipher 4

RC4, also known as ARC4 or ARCFOUR, is a widely used software encryption algorithm that employs the "stream cipher" construct. This algorithm is used in the web-based secure socket layer (SSL) protocol as well as the wired equivalent privacy (WEP). RC4 was designed in 1987 by Ron Rivest of RSA Security. RC4 was kept a trade secret until September 1994, when a description of the process was posted at an Internet mailing list. This was followed quickly by postings to a newsgroup, and from there it propagated to many Internet web sites. Once the process was known, it was no longer a trade secret. However, RSA has never officially released the algorithm. Unofficial implementations, usually referred to as ARC4 (alleged RC4) are considered by many to be legal since they do not use the RC4 trademarked name.

It is instructive to consider the operation of RC4 in the WEP application. In configuring a wireless access point that employs WEP encryption, the owner creates a "preshared" key. This is usually a five- or thirteen-character key. During operation, the WEP system creates a packet-specific key consisting of three additional characters selected at random. These are appended to the characters of the preshared key to create a secret key that will be used to encrypt the packet. This packet-specific three-character key is called the initialization vector (IV). For example, if the preshared key consisted of the character-string "tests," the WEP algorithm might append an IV of "abc" to create the secret key of the first packet, "abctests." This secret key is used to encrypt the packet following the process described below. The second data packet, however, will use a different IV—the secret key for the second packet might be "deftests." This process continues throughout the transmission of the data.

The secret key is used by a process called the key scheduling algorithm (KSA) to create a pseudo-random state array. This array resembles the permutation array described above in Table 2.1. Since the secret key changes with each data packet, the permutation array also changes with each packet.

Finally, a pseudo-random number generator (PRG) uses the KSA's random state array to create a streaming key. This streaming key is merged with the plain-text data to create an encrypted output stream. Like the one-time pad described above, the merging process uses an exclusive-OR process (XOR) that combines a bit from the input (the plain-text file) and a corresponding bit from the key stream to produce the encrypted output bit.

The WEP implementation of RC4 adds a cyclic redundancy checksum (CRC) value to the end of the data packet. Calculated from the accumulated sum of the bits in the packet, the CRC allows the receiving party to know that that packet has not been altered or otherwise corrupted during transmission. Once the packet is received, the appended CRC is removed and a new CRC value calculated based on the received data. The two CRC values should match. If not, the packet is discarded.

Finally, the IV is appended in plain text to the encrypted data. The flow chart in Figure 2.3 summarizes the RC4 encryption process.

The decryption process on the receiving end proceeds as follows. When a packet is received, the plaintext IV is removed and merged with the preshared password to create the same secret key that was used in the encryption process. This key is used by KSA to create a duplicate pseudo-random state array that is then used by the PRG to create the same streaming key that was used for encryption. The streaming key is XORed with the encrypted text, which produces the plain text and the CRC value. The CRC

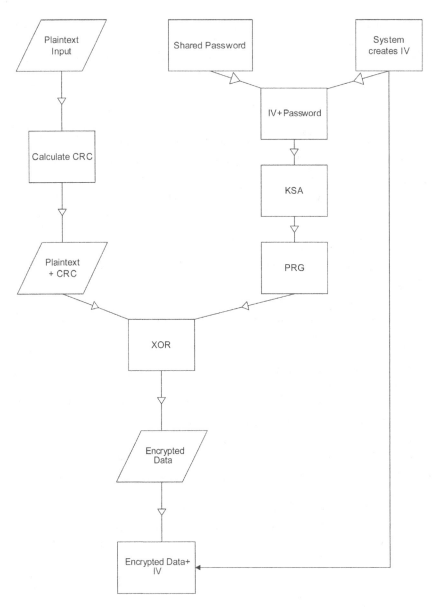

**Figure 2.3** RC4 encryption process.

is removed and a new CRC calculated—if the two match, the decryption was good and not altered. If there is no match, the packet is discarded.

The RC4 decryption process is summarized in Figure 2.4.

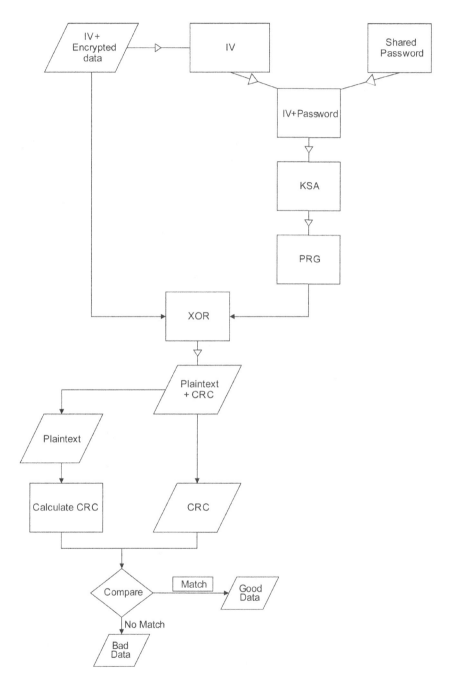

**Figure 2.4** RC4 decryption process.

RC4 has several weaknesses that create attack points for hackers. Three of these weaknesses are apparent from the process described above, and others have become apparent by deeper investigation. The first three attack points employ the following facts that can be gleaned from the process itself:

- The IV is sent as plain text appended to the encrypted packet. This can easily be obtained by anyone using a packet sniffer, and so the first three characters of the secret key are known at the outset.
- The KSA and PRG processes have predictable behaviors in the first few steps of their algorithms. This, combined with the knowledge of the first three characters of the secret key, creates vulnerability for the RC4 process.
- The XOR process involves an input string, a key stream, and an output string. Due to its nature, XOR is easily used to determine a third element if the other two are known.

Deeper research has revealed additional weaknesses in RC4:

- A hacker has a one in twenty chance of guessing what will happen during the KSA process.
- The first value of RC4's encrypted data is a hexadecimal "AA." As a result, sniffing the first byte of encrypted text and performing an XOR operation with hex AA allows the determination of the first output byte produced by the PRG.
- The IV used in the WEP process is susceptible to certain "weak" formats that are subject to cracking. These are referred to as "weak initialization vectors."

In light of these weaknesses, RC4 is generally considered a less than ideal choice for systems that require strong security.

## Blowfish

Blowfish[3] is a symmetric block cipher that can be used as a replacement for DES or IDEA. It uses a variable-length key, from 32 bits to 448 bits, so it spans both domestic and exportable applications. Blowfish was designed in 1993 by Bruce Schneier as a fast, free alternative to existing encryption algorithms. Blowfish encrypts data in 8-byte blocks. The algorithm has two primary steps: a key-expansion step and a data-encryption step.

During the key-expansion process, Blowfish creates a "P-array" consisting of 18 32-bit subkeys and four 32-bit "S-boxes" with 256 entries each. Blowfish expands the key by using the digits of P1, which are used to initialize the P-array. Then P1 is XOR'd with the first 32 bits of the key, P2 is XOR'd with the second 32 bits of the key, etc. A similar process is used to create the S-array. Armed with the P and S arrays, the Blowfish algorithm can then be used for encryption and decryption. The Blowfish algorithm is summarized by the flow chart in Figure 2.5.

In Figure 2.5 the function F is an additional transformation function. The F function process is summarized in the flow chart in Figure 2.6.

As of 2008, there has been no successful attack on the full Blowfish algorithm short of brute force approaches. The 64-bit block size is considered potentially problematic due to the reduced guessing space of the birthday paradox (see below in this chapter). Larger block sizes are generally preferred, especially for encrypting large files.

### Advanced Encryption Standard

Advanced encryption standard (AES) is a symmetric key 128-bit block cipher that was adopted by NIST in November, 2001[4]. AES is also sometimes referred to as Rijndael after the algorithm upon which it is based. Rijndael was developed by two Belgian cryptographers, Joan Daemen and Vincent Rijmen and is a broader implementation of the algorithm than the AES standard, which has a fixed block size of 128 bits and key sizes of 128, 192, or 256 bits.

In the AES algorithm, there is an input block, an output data block, and a 128-bit key. The 128-bit input block is stored in a 4-x-4 array of bytes and given the name "state." All the operations are done on this state array. The key is also put into a 4-x-4 array of bytes. During the encryption or decryption process, the original key is used to create "round keys," one for each "round" or iteration. The algorithm has four functions: add round key, sub bytes, shift row, and mix column. The specific details of each of these AES functions are beyond the scope of this book but can be found in a number of references[3, 5, 6]. There are 10 iterations of these functions during the encryption/decryption process. The final iteration (round) is a specialized round without the function mix column.

Figure 2.7 shows the flow chart of the AES encryption process.

The encryption algorithm upon which AES is based (Rijndael) has been designed using state-of-the-art knowledge of cryptographic research and is still believed to be very secure at the time of this writing (2008). However, new algebraic attacks have appeared.

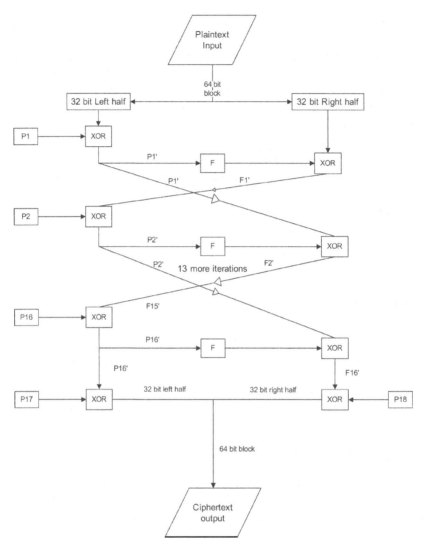

**Figure 2.5** Blowfish encryption process.

In a paper presented at Asiacrypt 2002[7], Nicolas Courtois and Josef Pieprzyk showed that AES can be written as an overdefined system of multivariate quadratic equations. By using a known plain-text input, the authors show that the task of recovering the 128-bit secret key can be

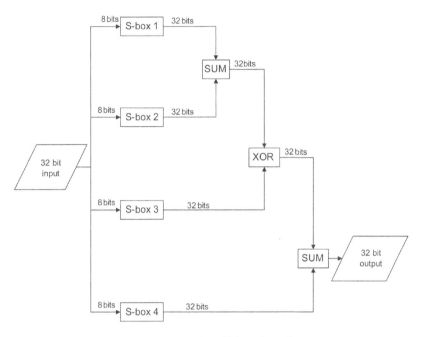

**Figure 2.6**  Blowfish F function.

expressed as a system of 8000 quadratic equations with 1600 unknowns. Solving such a large system of equations requires an efficient algorithm, and at this time no such algorithm has been demonstrated capable of obtaining a solution, although some have been proposed. This possibility of an attack has made AES a controversial topic at cryptanalysis meetings.

**Quantum Cryptography**

In 1984[8], two researchers, Charles H. Bennett, a fellow at IBM's Thomas J. Watson Research Center, and Gilles Brassard, a researcher at the University of Montreal in Canada, published a seminal paper in which they presented the core concept of quantum cryptography. This approach to secure sharing of a key for symmetric key cryptography employs a basic physical property of quantum mechanics as seen in light propagation.

At its heart, quantum cryptography takes advantage of an aspect of the Heisenberg uncertainty principle, which (paraphrased) states that the very act of observing a particle disturbs its state. More specifically, Heisenberg

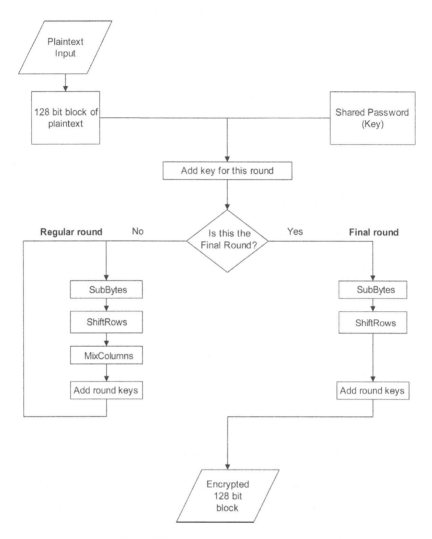

**Figure 2.7** AES encryption process.

stated that there are related properties of physical quanta such that the measurement of one property (such as position) destroys all information about the related property (such as momentum). When applied to photons, measuring an aspect such as polarization destroys the photon itself. Although not searching for a new cryptographic method, Bennett and Brassard realized that this one-way property is especially useful for key sharing in cryptography, since the receipt of a key transmitted by photons destroys the photons. Moreover, this property also allows the detection and prevention of any form of eavesdropping by a third party, since their presence would also destroy the photons. By the same token, photons received successfully by the intended party would no longer be available to an attacker for interception or sniffing.

In their study, Bennett and Brassard developed a method to transmit a key optically over a distance. In order to send a stream of "ones" and "zeroes" with certainty, it is not sufficient to construct a system in which the absence of a "one" is assumed to be a "zero," since the failure of the transmitter or receiver could produce a "zero" where it was not intended. Instead, a more robust system employs a scheme by which a "one" is sent by a transmitter as photon, and a "zero" is sent by the transmitter as a photon with a distinguishably different property. Polarization provides just such a property. By prior agreement, a photon that is (let's say) vertically polarized should be interpreted as a "one," and a photon that is diagonally polarized should be interpreted as a "zero." By using a polarizer and orienting it appropriately, the sender can transmit a stream of photons to a distant receiver that has complementary equipment to detect the polarization of an incoming photon. Since the photon and its polarization are destroyed upon measurement, interception or sniffing is not possible.

The "quantum" property of light is employed using the following principles. Light has a wave-particle duality. That is, depending on how the light is being measured, it can be considered to be a light wave or a particle. The wave nature of light is typically manifested in situations where interference phenomena are being examined (such as in single and double slit experiments and diffraction grating studies). The particle nature of light is typically used to explain phenomena when studying the interaction of light with materials (the optical ejection of electrons from a surface due to the photoelectric effect or detection using photodiodes and CCDs). As a light wave, a photon's polarization is determined by the orientation of the oscillating electric field to some external reference, such as a polarizing filter. If a photon's polarization is perpendicular to the orientation of a polarizing filter, it will not pass through the filter. In a particle representation, a polarized photon is said to carry angular momentum whose orientation is determined by the spin of the photon. If the photon's spin does not match the spin selectivity of the polarizing filter, the photon will not get through. (There are no partial photons, only an average of the total number of photons.)

If a photon encounters a polarizing filter that is oriented at 45 degrees to its polarization, there is a 50 percent probability that the photon will get through and a 50 percent probability that it will not. This embodiment of the Heisenberg uncertainty principle makes quantum cryptography strong. If the photon does get through the filter, its polarization upon exit will match the polarization of the filter—no information about its previous polarization survives. This process is said to "randomize" the polarization. In quantum cryptography, this property is employed to allow detection of eavesdropping. The destruction of the photon either by absorption on a detector or destruction in a crossed polarizer makes quantum cryptography a "one-way" process.

It is instructive to examine a basic implementation of quantum cryptography in which two people, typically referred to in the cryptography community as Alice and Bob, wish to share a key that can then be used in conventional symmetric key cryptography to exchange encrypted messages. In such a system, Alice and Bob are each equipped with two polarizers. One of these polarizers is aligned along a predefined north/south (for a "one") or east/west axis (for a "zero")—we will refer to this as the "+" basis. The second polarizer is oriented along either + 45 degrees (for a "one") or − 45 degrees (for a "zero") direction—we refer to this as the "x" basis. Alice can send a "one" to Bob by sending a photon with its polarization oriented along the "one" direction for either the + or x basis. Bob does not know in advance what Alice is sending—ones or zeroes—nor does he know which basis she is using for each. So Alice might send a stream of ones and zeroes as shown in Table 2.4.

Bob does not know what Alice will be sending, nor does he know which basis to use, so he selects at random the basis to which his receiving polarizer is set and records whether or not he observes a photon passing through. (Recall that a photon with a polarization oriented at 45 degrees to the receiving basis has a 50 percent chance of passing through the filter.)

Bob stores the result in an encrypted location on his computer and does not share it with anyone. He now communicates with Alice in the clear (that is, this may be overheard without risk), reporting the sequence of orientations that he used. She tells him which orientations should have allowed him to detect the polarization of the transmitted photon correctly.

**Table 2.4**   Alice's transmission.

| Photon polarization | \ | | | _ | / | \ | | | _ | _ | / | \ |
|---|---|---|---|---|---|---|---|---|---|---|
| Binary value | 0 | 1 | 0 | 1 | 0 | 1 | 0 | 0 | 1 | 0 |

**Table 2.5**   Bob's reception.

| Bit number | 1 | 2 | 3 | 4 | 5 | 6 | 7 | 8 | 9 | 10 |
|---|---|---|---|---|---|---|---|---|---|---|
| Alice's transmission | \ | \| | _ | / | \ | \| | _ | _ | / | \ |
| Alice's intended bits | 0 | 1 | 0 | 1 | 0 | 1 | 0 | 0 | 1 | 0 |
| Bob's filter orientation | / | \| | — | \| | / | \ | \| | \ | / | _ |
| Allowed orientations | √ | √ | √ |  | √ |  | √ |  | √ |  |
| Final result | 0 | 1 | 0 |  | 0 |  | 0 |  | 1 |  |

In Table 2.5, the result of this discussion is the "allowed orientations" list. Since Alice knows whether she sent a "one" or a "zero" for each of these allowed orientations, and Bob knows whether or not he observed a "one" or a "zero," the two parties now have a shared sequence of bits that they can use as a symmetric key to encrypt communications. Note that, on average, Bob will get a fraction of the orientations correct, so it is best to send longer strings of bits than the desired final key length in order to compensate for this.

The basic form of quantum cryptography described above could potentially be broken by a "man in the middle" attack. In such an attack, an eavesdropper, usually called "Eve," inserts herself into the middle of the conversation between Alice and Bob, measures the photons received from Alice, and retransmits photons to Bob. In principle, a successful man-in-the-middle attack, although difficult to implement in the direct connection environment required by quantum cryptography, could defeat the system.

More sophisticated forms of quantum cryptography have been developed to address such potential weaknesses[9,10]. "Entangled pairs" are pairs of photons that are created by specific elementary particle reactions. These photon pairs have different but related polarizations. The fact that they are "entangled" means that any measurement of one particle destroys the polarization correlation of the other. Applied to quantum cryptography, a sequence of entangled photons is created. Alice measures the polarization of one of each pair, and Bob measures the polarization of the other photon in the pair. Since the photon pairs are entangled, they will both measure the same polarization and obtain the same result. If an eavesdropper intercepts one of the photons in the transmission, she would have to also retransmit the result in order to remain hidden. However, this retransmitted photon will not be entangled with the original pair. Entanglement allows Alice and Bob to easily detect an eavesdropper.

## Hash Algorithms

A hash function is used to create a nonreversible, fixed-length message digest from any length of input string. The message digest (also called a hash or digital fingerprint) is fixed in length and must have two important qualities:

- It must be nonreversible—the computational task required to find the input string given a hash must be infeasible.
- The probability of finding a collision, in which two messages have the same message digest, must be vanishingly small.

If either of these qualities is not met, there would be a possibility of an attack in which an unauthorized message is substituted for the authorized message.

The basic process of a secure hash algorithm is shown in Figure 2.8. In this process, an input plain-text file is broken up into fixed blocks, and each block is sequentially compressed to a fixed size. The output of each step is then used as the chain variable for the next step, and the process is repeated until the entire input plain-text file has been processed. This produces a fixed-length message digest as shown in Figure 2.8.

### *The Birthday Paradox and Hash Algorithms*

At first glance, it would appear that the probability of guessing the hash message digest of an input plain-text file would be just the number of possible combinations of the bits in the message. For example, a 160-bit message digest has 2160 possible combinations of bits, and so a brute force attack should require guessing, on average, half that total number of combinations. But a mathematical process referred to as the birthday paradox asserts that the correct answer can be guessed with much fewer attempts.

The birthday paradox, in its original form, can be stated as follows. How many people must be in a room before two of them have the same birthday? One might think that it would take about half of 365, or 182 people. In actuality, when there are 20 people in a room, each of the 20 people is now asking each of the other 19 people about their birthdays. Each individual person only has a small (less than 5 percent) chance of success, but by asking the entire room, each person is effectively trying it 19 times. That increases the probability dramatically.

To develop a calculation of the exact probability, the following concept helps develop the expressions needed. Let's say there is a calendar with all 365 days on it. Person 1 walks in and put a big X on his birthday. The sec-

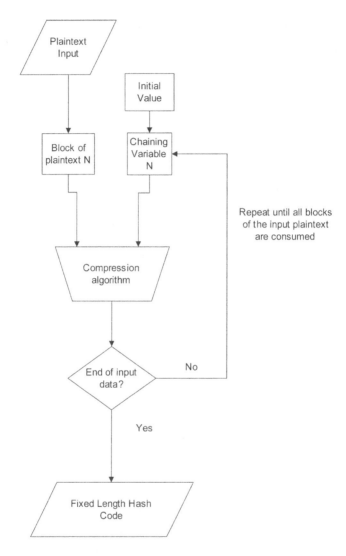

**Figure 2.8** General secure hash code process.

ond person who walks in has only one possible date for a match, so the probability of the two dates not colliding is (1- 1/365). The third person has two possible birthdays that his could match, so the probability of not colliding is (1- 2/365).

For a general case where the number of possible numbers (here this would be birthdays) is N, and the number of candidates for comparison (number of people in the room) is s, the formula becomes:

$$P_{\text{no match}}(N,s) = [(1\text{-}1/N) \times (1\text{-}2/N) \times (1\text{-}3/N) \cdots \times (1\text{-}(s\text{-}1)/N]$$

Replacing 1 with N/N, this becomes:

$$P_{\text{no match}}(N,s) = [(N\text{-}1)/N \times (N\text{-}2)/N \times (N\text{-}3)/N \cdots \times (N\text{-}(s\text{-}1)/N]$$

Regrouping terms:

$$P_{\text{no match}}(N,s) = [(N\text{-}1)*(N\text{-}2)*(N\text{-}3) \cdots *(N\text{-}(s\text{-}1)]/N^s$$

This can be recognized as:

$$P_{\text{no match}}(N,s) = \frac{N!}{(N\text{-}s)! * N^s}$$

So the probability of a match is 1-P no match:

$$P_{\text{no match}}(N,s) = 1 - \frac{N!}{(N\text{-}s)! * N^s}$$

For large N (N > 100), Stirling's approximation can be used, and this becomes:

Equation 2.1          $$P_{\text{match}}(N,s) \approx e^{-s(s\text{-}1)/2N}$$

For the birthday paradox, N = 365 and s is unknown (basically, we are trying to answer the question of how many people must be in a room before a birthday match is likely?). We can choose the probability of a match to be relatively high, say, 50 percent. Taking the natural log of both sides, this equation becomes:

$$\ln(1/2) = s(s\text{-}1)/2*365$$

$$730 * (\text{-}0.693) = s(s\text{-}1)$$

$$\text{Or } s^2 \text{ - } s + 507 = 0$$

Solving the quadratic equation, we find that for a probable match of 50 percent, we need s = 23 people in the room.

Say an attacker tries a one-way hash function, producing a hash of size n bits. Using a brute force guessing approach, the attacker will need to try $2^n$ random messages to get a message that produces a specific hash value. SHA-1 (160 bit digests) requires $1.4 \times 10^{48}$ guesses. The fastest super-computer today can perform 12 teraflops ($1.2 \times 10^{13}$ flops = floating point operations per second). If the supercomputer could magically calcu-late a SHA-1 guess in one flop, this brute force guessing process would yield a match in $4 \times 10^{27}$ years.

Now let's use the birthday-paradox approach to find two random mes-sages M1 and M2, which can give the same hash value h. This will be analogous to trying to find two people with the same birthday. Using Equation 2.1 above, where $N = 2^{160}$, we find a probable match using a birthday attack with $s = 1.4 \times 10^{24}$ guesses. Again, if the supercomputer could magically calculate a SHA-1 guess in one flop, this brute force guessing process would yield a match in 2777 years, significantly less than our initial estimate.

A complementary critical component of cryptography, key generation and distribution, is discussed in Chapter 3. Together, Chapters 2 and 3 pro-vide the necessary basis for examining various hardware-based approaches to computer security that will be discussed in the balance of this book.

## REFERENCES

[1] National Bureau of Standards, *Data Encryption Standard, Federal Information Processing Standards Publication (FIPS PUB) 46-1*. U.S. Department of Commerce, 1977. Reaffirmed 1988.

[2] American National Standards Institute, *Data Encryption Algorithm, ANSI X3.92-1981*, 1980.

[3] Proceedings of the First Fast Software Encryption workshop in Cambridge, UK, (published by Springer-Verlag, *Lecture Notes in Computer Science #809*, 1994).

[4] National Institute of Standards and Technology, U.S. Department of Commerce, *"The Advanced Encryption Standard,"* Federal Information Processing Standards Publication 197, Washington, D.C., November 2001.

[5] J. Daemen and V. Rijmen. The Design of Rijndael, *AES—The Advanced Encryption Standard*, Springer-Verlag, 2002.

[6] N. Ferguson, J. Kelsey, B. Schneier, M. Stay, D. Wagner, and D. Whiting. "Improved cryptanalysis of Rijndael." In B. Schneier, editor, *Proceedings of Fast Software Encryption 2000*, LNCS, Springer-Verlag, 2000, pp. 213–230.

7  N. Courtois, J. Pieprzyk, Cryptanalysis of block ciphers with overdefined sys-
   tems of equations. Lecture Notes in Computer Science, Vol. 2501, Y. Zhang
   (Ed), Asiacrypt 2002, 8th International Conference on the Theory and
   Applications of Cryptology and Information Security, Queenstown, New
   Zealand, December 2002, Proceedings, Springer, pp. 267–287.

8  Bennett C. H. and Brassard G., 1984 *Proceedings, IEEE International
   Conference on Computers, Systems, and Signal Processing* (New York, New
   York, IEEE, 1984,) pp. 175–9.

9  A. K. Ekert, *Physical Review*, Letters, 67, 661 (1991).

10 A. K. Ekert, J. G. Rarity, P. R. Tapster, and G. M. Palma, *Physical Review*,
   Letters, 69, 1293 (1992).

# Chapter 3

## KEY GENERATION AND DISTRIBUTION APPROACHES AND ATTACKS

Just as encryption is central to computer security, the generation and sharing of a cryptographic key (sometimes referred to as a password) are central to encryption. Unlike encryption algorithms, which can be difficult to break, the cryptographic key is a central point of attack. A hacker who obtains the cryptographic key for an encrypted file or session has complete access to the information contained therein. Therefore the key (and its handling) must be made as strong as possible. The creation and sharing of strong keys is a critical part of a secure system, and failure to perform either task well can determine the ultimate security of the system.

### KEY GENERATION

An ideal key (or "password") is completely random; it is as large as allowed by the system; and its characters span the entire possible character space, including numbers and special characters. Unfortunately, keys with these characteristics cannot easily be memorized by a user. Cryptographic systems usually place the responsibility for entering the key in the hands of the user. Referred to by some as "something you know," the concept is that, to the extent that the key is difficult to guess and to the extent that the user keeps the key secret, the system should be secure. Entering complex keys, however, can be taxing for users, especially if they are required to memorize several such keys or change them frequently, as may be required by organizational policy. Because of the memorization requirement, keys usually are constructed to be easily recalled. This often creates an unfortunate susceptibility to various forms of dictionary attacks.

Recalling the discussion on average attack space in Chapter 1, the larger the attack space (the average number of guesses that must be made to guess a key), the stronger the key. In general, the total number of possible combinations of a key of N bits is $2^N$. The shorter the key, the fewer the possible combinations of characters that comprise it and therefore the easier it is to guess the key. As explained in Chapter 2, 56-bit (7-character) keys are considered weak by today's standards.

The previously mentioned study by psychology researchers at Cambridge University[1] reveals that weak passwords occur quite frequently. Weak passwords, by the study's definition, were characterized by their ease of guessing. The study found that passwords created randomly were the strongest, though often hard to memorize. Interestingly, the study also revealed that passwords based on mnemonic phrases are just as hard to crack as passwords that are generated by random generators. They cite an example of a password created from a mnemonic: "My sister Peg is 24 years old" would create MsPi24yo.

Attacks on keys (passwords) generally fall into five basic categories:

- Dictionary attacks, in which words found in the dictionary are tried
- Permutation attacks, in which dictionary words are appended with some small (1 through 4) number of digits
- Substitution attacks, in which certain letters are replaced with numbers or common special characters ("viscous" might become "v1Scou$", for example)
- User information, in which basic information about the user, such as first, middle, or last name, initials, pet's name, spouse's name, etc., are tried
- Brute force (trying all possible combinations of allowed characters)

The birthday paradox, described in Chapter 2, demonstrates that even the brute force method will likely not take as long as one might imagine (although it is generally the method of last resort). The continued development of more powerful supercomputers (as well as the promise of revolutionary technologies such as quantum computing) may make the brute force approach more attractive over time.

It is critical that strong keys be generated and employed wherever security is required. The generation of strong keys can be accomplished in several ways. If key generation is left as a task for the user, the Cambridge University study cited above suggests that creating long keys by using mnemonics is the best choice. The use of random generators is a second choice, although their output does not always lend itself to easy memorization by a user.

There are two basic types of random-number generators: pseudo-random number generators (PRGs), and hardware-based random-number generators (RNGs). Each generates random sequences of bits in which each bit is statistically independent of the other, much like a fair coin used in a coin toss. This produces a uniform distribution of ones and zeroes, which can be combined to produce numbers of some selected size (such as 32 bits, for example).

The output of both types of random-number generators must be analyzed carefully before the generator is employed in cryptographic applications. Repeating a requirement presented in Chapter 1, key generators must pass two tests:

- Test 1: Does the output have any discernable pattern?
- Test 2: Can the generator be forced to reproduce its output by resetting initial conditions or through the introduction of external manipulation?

**Software Key Generation**

Algorithms that are used to generate cryptographic keys are pseudo-random number generators that produce output that spans the allowed space for cryptographic keys (such as letters, numbers, and certain special characters, for example). Most PRGs are tested thoroughly to assure that they do not have discernable patterns or other fatal repetitive signatures (test 1 above) that might be used to predict or reverse the generated output. But, as explained in Chapter 1, a concern about PRGs is that they can be placed in a predictable state.

One test to determine whether or not a PRG has a discernable pattern in its output involves examining the distribution of the output. It is desirable that the output be as unbiased in frequency as possible. Even though a PRG may produce a random output without discernable patterns, the output may have statistical biases over a large number of samples. This bias is most easily observed by plotting the power spectrum of the output for a large sample of numbers generated by the PRG. A PRG is said to produce white noise if the spectral density of its output is flat as a function of frequency.

Physics and engineering disciplines often employ power-spectrum analysis (similar to an autocorrelation test) in order to determine the spectral properties of a signal or set of data. In this analysis, a Fourier transform of the data is performed, the zero frequency (DC offset) suppressed, and the log of the square of the magnitude of the transform plotted as a function of frequency. This power spectrum ideally should be flat and relatively featureless. An example of such a flat (or white-noise) spectrum is shown in Figure 3.1.

Some noise sources display $1/f$ dependence in the distribution of the output. That is, the noise (sometimes referred to as "pink noise") is biased

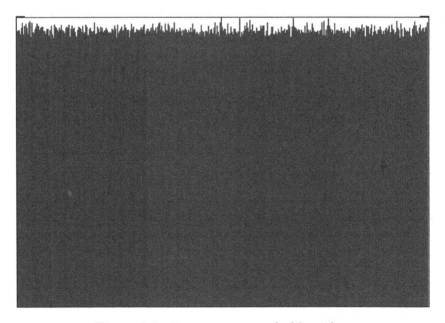

**Figure 3.1**   Power spectrum of white noise.

more towards lower frequencies and less towards higher frequencies. Such a bias would indicate that the noise source is more likely to favor one range of values over another, thereby possibly reducing the attack space.

A power-spectrum analysis can be used to reveal the presence of additional undesirable characteristics. For example, a noise source might have a defect that causes it to produce a certain value once every minute. Such a defective noise source will display a power spectrum with multiple spikes, representing the higher harmonics of the fixed pattern. The power spectrum of a white-noise source that repeats a fixed number after some fixed amount of time (say, every 10 seconds) is shown in Figure 3.2.

A noise source might have a sine wave or other type of periodic function superimposed on it, perhaps due to outside interference or defects in assembly. An example of the power spectrum of a white-noise source that has a pure sine wave of 2 percent of the total noise amplitude added to it is shown in Figure 3.3.

The power spectrum, derived from the Fourier transform of the data, displays the "power" present at each frequency that is observed within that

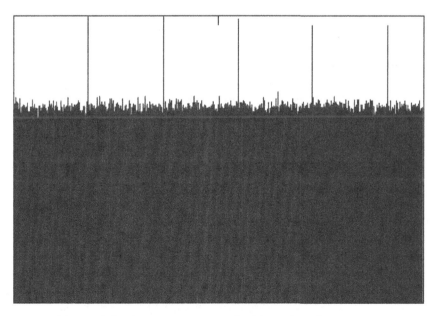

**Figure 3.2**    Power spectrum of white noise plus pattern.

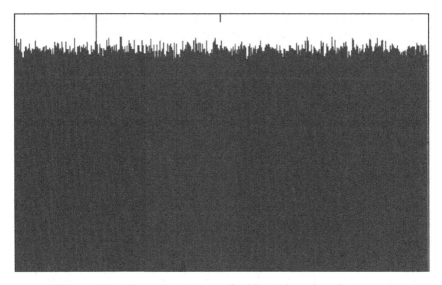

**Figure 3.3**   Power spectrum of white noise plus sine wave.

data. In the example above, where a single pure sine wave has been added to otherwise white noise, a single spike is produced in the power spectrum, corresponding to the frequency of the added sine wave.

A PRG is an algorithm, and as such, is ultimately predictable. It may take time and effort to predict the outcome of such a process, but it can be defeated. An attack on a PRG is usually accomplished by placing the PRG in a predictable (initial) state. Knowledge of the initial state or, alternatively, placing the PRG in a fixed initial state, can be used to give control of the cryptographic key to an attacker. For example, a PRG might use the system clock as a source of a changing seed. In principle, the cryptographic keys created using this system would be different each time the PRG is invoked. Placement of a Trojan horse that resets the system clock to a fixed initial value each time the PRG is invoked or otherwise intercepts the software request for clock time and replaces it with a fixed value would create a completely predictable system.

A PRG might store the previous seed in a file and then add an offset each time, thereby changing the initial conditions. Replacement or deletion of the seed file would place the PRG in a known state, thereby allowing control by an attacker. It is difficult to construct a cryptographic key generator based on a pseudo-random number generator that will pass test 2.

For this reason, hardware-based cryptographic key generators are gaining in popularity; they often can pass both tests. To the extent that hardware generators have "clean" power spectra, they are usually superior to PRGs.

## Hardware Key Generation

Hardware-based random-number generators are generally small devices that employ some physical process to produce random numbers. The degree to which the output is random is easily subjected to independent tests, and several such devices have been employed to create cryptographic keys. The specific physical processes employed to generate random numbers include noise (shot noise or thermal noise), quantum processes, and timing approaches. (Secure tokens that employ numbers that change every minute are employed as part of a two-factor authentication system and will be discussed in a subsequent chapter on authentication.)

### *Noise-Based Approaches*

There are two fundamental types of electronic noise: thermal (or Johnson-Nyquist) noise and shot noise. Thermal noise arises from the agitation of current carriers due to ambient temperature effects and is independent of whether or not an external voltage is applied to the device. Reduction of this noise is the reason that some radio and optical astronomy telescopes cool their receivers for extremely low signal-level measurements. Thermal noise is an example of white noise (its power spectrum is flat as a function of frequency). Thermal noise does not have its origins in a quantum mechanical process but rather in stochastic processes governed by the laws of thermodynamics.

Shot noise, in contrast, arises from fluctuations in the number of current carriers. These fluctuations arise from the fact that current carriers are discrete units (usually electrons) that are subject to statistical fluctuations in their numbers from moment to moment. Although the long-term average number of carriers arriving per unit of time may be constant, specific samples of the instantaneous number of carriers arriving per unit of time varies according to Poisson statistics. This variation is the source of shot noise.

### *Noisy Diodes and Resistors*

Thermal noise is the most easily measured of the above approaches. One such implementation is avalanche noise, in which the breakdown noise generated by a zener diode operating in reverse bias mode is measured. These devices are somewhat susceptible to physical attack if the device is cooled. Thermal noise decreases with temperature, and in some cases such devices will stop operating entirely if they are cooled sufficiently. A resistor at room temperature will generate noise that can be detected with amplification. As with zener diodes, a random-number generator based on this approach is susceptible to physical attack in which the temperature is lowered. The difficulty of gaining access to such a device and lowering its temperature without detection is significant but should not be discounted for nation-state attacks that have nearly unlimited resources. It should be noted that some assert that random numbers from thermal sources are not truly random, since they are not derived from a quantum-mechanical process.

*Radio-Frequency Sources*
The radio-frequency (RF) spectrum provides various opportunities to collect noise. A radio tuned to 160 Gigahertz ("GHz") will receive noise from the thermal remnant of the cosmological birth of the universe (the "big bang"). Other frequencies can receive electrostatic discharge noise from lightning, although this is not strictly thermal in origin. Use of the power-spectrum-analysis approach described above can reveal the extent to which a measured process has the desirable flat spectrum.

These types of passive listening devices can possibly be attacked by operating a transmitter (tuned to the device's frequency) in the vicinity of the receiver, thereby overpowering the weaker noise measurements with a deterministic signal. Only differential RF receiver approaches can offer some degree of immunity to this type of attack.

*Brownian-Motion Devices*
Brownian motion of particles due to impact by air molecules, while not technically a quantum-mechanical process in its own right, is a probabilistic process based on the collision of large numbers of atomic-scale quanta with a macroscopic particle. In 1827, Scottish botanist Robert Brown[2] observed a curious phenomenon while examining pollen under a microscope. The phenomenon, later named Brownian motion, became the impetus for a breakthrough work by Albert Einstein[3] nearly 80 years later. In his paper, Einstein explained that these random movements arise from a stochastic bombardment of the small particle by atoms and molecules in the surrounding medium. Occasionally, Einstein explained, statistical fluctuations from atoms can add up to produce a large enough impulsive force to cause the much larger particle to move a macroscopic distance. This gives rise to the apparent random movement of the pollen. The stochastic process that governs Brownian motion produces an unbiased source of noise.

Einstein's calculations also showed that the mean radial distance that a particle will travel due to Brownian motion is proportional to the square root of the temperature.

Since Brownian motion has temperature dependence, it is not generally considered a good candidate for hardware-based random-number generation due to the requirement to control temperature in order to avoid biased noise output.

### Quantum Devices

In addition to the randomness produced by the two types of electronic noise described above, quantum mechanics also predicts that various physical phenomena are completely random. As an example, the theory predicts (and empirical measurements confirm) that the time between subsequent decays of a nuclear decay process (used in some types of smoke detectors, for example) is random. Certain optical approaches also have an output that is random and determined by the uncertainty principle of quantum mechanics. If properly implemented, each of these can be used to produce unbiased random numbers.

#### Nuclear Decay Devices

In quantum mechanics, the probability that an atom in an excited state will decay (radioactively) to a more stable state is random, unpredictable, and independent of other events around the atom. When such a transition occurs, a beta particle (a high-speed electron) is emitted. A detector can be constructed that consists of an appropriately chosen gas placed between two electrodes to which a high voltage is applied. When a beta particle from such a nuclear decay enters the chamber, it collides with a gas molecule, which then is ionized into positive and negative ions, which then are drawn to the electrodes by the electric field. As the ions travel, they too collide with other molecules. A rapid chain reaction (an avalanche) occurs in which many ions are created, all drifting to (and ultimately collected by) the electrodes. Detection electronics attached to the electrodes then observe a pulse of current, which can be used to mark the time of the nuclear decay.

It has been theorized and confirmed by observation that the time between successive decays is random. A power-spectrum analysis of the decay times measured in this fashion is shown in Figure 3.4.

The key point to observe is that the power spectrum is flat as a function of frequency. Due to the small size of the data, the spectrum has more noise than previous spectral plots, but the flat feature remains apparent. Such a source of random numbers is ideal for cryptographic applications.

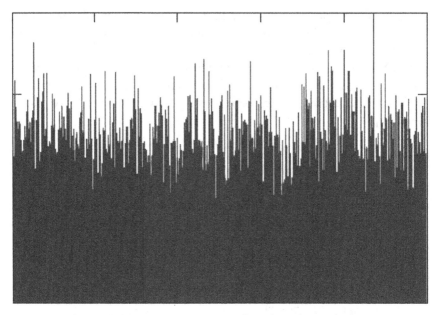

**Figure 3.4**   Power spectrum of nuclear decay timings.

The recent development of small, solid-state decay detectors makes the technology attractive for use in a PC.

An attack on this type of device would have to be mounted at one of two levels. First, since the device probably resides on a port or in a slot on the motherboard, a Trojan horse could possibly be inserted to circumvent the data being returned by the device and replace it with compromised data. This could be avoided by digitally signing the data. Second, a physical modification or replacement of the hardware device itself might go undetected, but this would require sufficient time and access to the board. As above, digitally signing the data would allow detection of the modification. Moreover, the use of a proprietary tamper-evident seal would further reduce the likelihood of such a successful attack. This type of random-number generator remains an attractive option for those requiring true random numbers.

*Optical Devices*
Quantum cryptography, described in Chapter 2, presents a recent addition to the family of device-based random-number generators. At the time of

this writing, two U.S. companies offer second-generation quantum cryptography products, and many of the top academic, government, and commercial research institutions have development efforts underway. In the opinion of top researchers at the National Security Agency, quantum cryptography appears to be unbreakable. The use of techniques such as entangled photons provides assurance against eavesdropping that is unmatched by other technologies.

Due to the apparent fundamental strength of quantum cryptography, future attacks on the technology will likely be limited to brute force attacks by powerful computers (such as quantum computers) or perhaps physical threats to authorized parties.

### *Other Hardware Sources of Randomness*

Another class of hardware-based random-number generators does not employ physics but rather uses mechanical or other environmentally available sources for noise. This class of random-number generators includes the measurement of user-specific keystroke timing, mouse movements, and disk-drive timings.

Attack avenues for these approaches are somewhat sophisticated but can include the introduction of Trojan-horse software modules that change the timings being reported to the system in order to alter its spectral properties, thereby making the generator more predictable.

Two of these hardware approaches (keystroke timings or mouse movements) usually employ an external unit that is attached to a PC through an IO or USB port, supplying random output to the PC on demand. An attack on such a device, short of altering the device itself, would be to either employ a Y connector (feeding predetermined numbers on demand in place of the true random numbers) or employing a software attack to replace the output stream on the IO port itself with a stream that has known characteristic timings independent of the user's movements.

## KEY DISTRIBUTION

As described in Chapter 2, symmetric key cryptography requires the secure distribution of the shared key or key generator, whereas asymmetric key cryptography does not. This section will be limited to cryptographic systems that require secure sharing of keys or key generators and will not address asymmetric key cryptography.

The distribution of keys or key generators consists of some or all of the following steps:

1. Creation
2. Initialization
3. Distribution
4. Authentication
5. Storage
6. Use

As an example, a simple symmetric system that uses a single static key will employ steps 1, 3, 5, and 6 (creation of the key, its distribution, its storage, and its use). A more complex system that employs a key generator (which is used to create one or more keys after distribution) would employ all six steps.

## Key Distribution for Software-Based PRGs

Creation and initialization of keys (and their consequent weaknesses and attack paths) have been discussed elsewhere. This section will focus on steps 3 through 6.

### *Key Distribution*

PRG (software)-based symmetric key systems have two basic distribution options for a shared key or key generator:

- The key/generator can be issued to a user in person.
- The key/generator can be transmitted to the user (electronically or on portable media).

The first option offers some degree of confidence that a user logging in will be authentic, since the user's identity can be confirmed during the issuing process. However, the administration of this process in a large organization may pose some challenges. Of greater concern is the protection of the key/generator by the user after issuing.

The second option greatly reduces the administrative overhead created by in-person issuing but immediately adds risk through uncertainty about the user's authenticity. Banks and credit agencies employ a two-step process and a back channel to reduce this risk, sending a credit card (for example) through the mail and then using either email or requiring an activation call to complete the process, thereby modestly raising the degree of difficulty for persons masquerading as others. Software companies employ a similar process for delivery of product. But unless some independent confirmation of a user's identity is performed on the receiving end of the process, the confidence in that person's identity is low, and the risk for a secure system is high.

The use of the second option for PRG key distribution is susceptible to interception (both electronically and through physical delivery channels such as the mail). Once an interception has occurred, the only task remaining for an attacker is to intercept the confirmation process. A sophisticated attacker could introduce a replacement pair to the user so that he now has established a means to observe or otherwise control the use of the system.

### *Key Storage*

Storing a file (such as a key) of any type using encryption involves the use of a separate cryptographic key, which is later used to decrypt the file. The key used for storing must also be protected, and if done so using encryption, it requires a key, and the process repeats without closure. It is best to use a long key that has been derived using strong cryptographic principles and to employ best practices (antivirus, antispyware, etc.) to protect the host operating system. However, storing a key that has its origins in a PRG has well-defined risks and is usually not considered acceptable to matters of national security.

Storage of a key generator, in contrast, requires that the generator (generally an executable or DLL) be stored in the clear in order to make its functions available. As explained in the attack section of PRGs earlier in this book, such functions can be compromised by known techniques and should not be used for high-security situations.

### *Key Use*

Improper use of a software key by a user is a common security risk. Users are inclined to write down passwords to avoid the requirement of memorization and tend to store the software keys in the clear on their computer, usually in a convenient (and often unencrypted) location. Post-it notes or key files that contain commonly used keys, PINs, passwords, and any other techniques to facilitate recall, other than the use of a mnemonic, must be strongly discouraged. Any such file that is stored on a computer or other device is potentially open to attack. Security holes in the operating system or firewall, the use of Trojan horses and key-capture techniques, cryptanalysis attacks, commandeering of a PRG through resetting of initial conditions, and other avenues all raise the risk of using a PRG.

The many security issues and attack avenues present for software-generated keys make the use of this type of key unacceptable for situations that demand the best possible protection of information through security.

## Key Distribution for Hardware-Based RNGs

### Creation of RNGs

The requirement that an RNG be physically manufactured offers a variety of opportunities for the designers to design security features and self-consistency checks directly into the device. (See the section on minimizing hardware attacks below.) The use of these techniques can virtually eliminate any security concerns regarding theft, spoofing, or even counterfeiting.

### Initialization of RNGs

The initial condition issues that dominate the software-based PRG key generators are more manageable for hardware-based RNGs, since such key generators cannot be forced into a compromising state. In addition, RNGs eliminate most of the security concerns relating to improper handling of the device after receipt, since, unlike PRGs, the hardware-based generators are not susceptible to software and operating-system attacks.

### Distribution of RNGs

Hardware-based RNGs require the physical delivery of the device itself, so the distribution options specified above still apply, but the second option is limited to transmission of the device itself through some trusted delivery service, such as the mail or other parcel services. (Optical cryptography using entangled photons presents an entirely different delivery situation, since it requires an optical path with specific properties between the transmitter and the receiver.)

It should be clear to the reader that the first distribution option for RNGs (issuing in person) is inherently more trustworthy than is delivery on portable media, since there is no reliance on a third party. The use of a back channel (email, telephone, signature, etc.) remains an option for validation of receipt of the device by the intended user, but it lacks the complete control over the process afforded by personal delivery, which remains the more secure of the two delivery options.

### Key Storage and Use

Proper use of protection offered by the physical device (described in the subsequent section) can eliminate or dramatically reduce security vulnerabilities that plague PRGs in the storage and use of keys, since key storage on an RNG can be encrypted and the device itself protected against hardware attacks.

## Minimizing Hardware Attack Risks

Many of the concerns associated with software-generated keys and their distribution can be reduced or eliminated by taking advantage of capabilities available to hardware-based key generators due to their being anchored in the physical world:

- These generators can be stored in a read-only environment, such as in the encrypted chip of a smart card. As optical resolution of the lithographic process (used in the manufacture of chips) gets smaller, it becomes significantly harder for attackers to apply physical attacks that might allow electronic measurement of the contents of these chips. The cost and time required to mount such an attack is becoming prohibitive except for the most valuable of target secrets.

- Tamper-evident technology can be employed to alert the user to unauthorized attempts to access a hardware-based RNG. Proper constraints on the sources of such labels can prevent attackers from obtaining copies. Entangled photons of the sort used in quantum cryptography have a form of tamper evidence and protection built into the technology at the level of quantum-mechanical processes. At the time of writing, it is widely believed that this technology cannot be defeated.

- Digital signing of the output can be performed securely within the protected physical space of the device, where access to internal modules is not provided to the outside world.

- Channel challenge/response authentication can be employed to eliminate counterfeiting. During initialization of a device, a large table can be filled with RNG-generated random numbers, and a copy of the table stored on the issuing server. During login, a challenge/response process can be used in which a message digest of the table can be requested of the device. Upon successful presentation of the correct message digest (reflecting the fact that the contents of the table are as expected), new RNG data can be sent to the user's device from the server in an encrypted channel, and the two tables updated for the next challenge/response. This system can be as strong as the encryption. Large keys and physical storage thereof can make this a very secure implementation.

In conclusion, hardware solutions offer advantages that are unavailable to software-only implementations of security. Software based key generation suffers from the predictability inherent in algorithmically based PRGs. Key sharing (especially for symmetric key cryptography) introduces additional opportunities for attack that can be mitigated by careful employment of hardware devices. As computing power increases, the time required to guess cryptographic keys will decrease dramatically, and any element of predictability present in a security system will accelerate the decrease. Hardware offers the best option for strong security in the long term, especially if the technologies employed minimize the use of algorithms and static identifiers. The subsequent chapters examine various additional hardware approaches that offer superior security against attacks and hackers.

## REFERENCES

[1] Yan, J, Blackwell, A., Anderson, R., Grant, A., "The Memorability and Security of Passwords," in Cranor, L.F., Garfinkel, S., eds., *Security and Usability*, 2005, p. 129.

[2] R. Brown, "A brief account of microscopical observations made in the months of June, July, and August, 1827, on the particles contained in the pollen of plants; and on the general existence of active molecules in organic and inorganic bodies," *Philosophical Magazine* 4, 161–173 s1828d; 6, 161–166 s1829d; Edinb. New Philos. J. 5, 358–371 s1828d.

[3] A. Einstein, "Über die von der molekularkinetischen Theorie der Wärme geforderte Bewegung von in ruhenden Flüssigkeiten suspendierten Teilchen," *Annals of Physics* 17, 549–560 s1905d.

# Chapter 4

## THE QUALITIES OF WORKABLE
## SECURITY SOLUTIONS

The preceding chapters have introduced two important points:

- Pure software security solutions are fraught with attack points and inherent weaknesses.

- Hardware-based security technologies dramatically reduce or eliminate those weaknesses through the introduction of non-algorithmic processes that are truly random. To the extent that these hardware devices can be physically secured against tampering, they can offer significantly stronger overall system security when combined with carefully developed software.

Any security-based application must employ both hardware and software and not rely solely upon software. Software is just an application, and therefore it can be broken.

Over time, key players in the computer-security field have been migrating more towards hardware-based solutions in order to supply their customers with secure systems that protect their mission-critical information and reduce risks due to loss, theft, or hacking. These solutions introduce a variety of approaches that implement the advantages offered by hardware-based security.

It is important to note, however, that just because a security element is implemented on a device, the implementation does not by itself guarantee improved security. Attack vectors for each of the following approaches will be presented in a manner similar to that of the preceding chapters.

## SECURE COPROCESSORS

Any security system must be constructed with the assumption that the device (and the data it is protecting) can be physically stolen. The protection of sensitive information, therefore, must be as strong as possible against unencumbered attacks, electronic and physical, that might occur in the privacy of an attacker's lab. One of the approaches to provide sufficient security against such events is the use of secure coprocessors.

A secure coprocessor is a separate (additional) processor that is attached to a host and has several characteristics:

- It is tamper-resistant and tamper-evident.
- It contains a cryptographic engine and factory-installed keys that are not visible or available to the outside world.
- Keys usually can be "zeroized" (erased) in response to an internal or external stimulus, such as an attack.

By isolating the cryptographic engine and its keys from the host, the secure coprocessor establishes an autonomous identity that cannot be defeated or compromised without detection even if the host has been compromised. This autonomous hardware device can be used to provide trusted authentication of its identity and any of its computational cryptographic results (through the use of a digital signature). Ideally, a secure processor will have both secure and nonsecure input/output channels that are rigorously separated from one another.

The secure coprocessor usually can run encrypted programs and protect data from unauthorized access. As a coprocessor, it has the added benefit that it can offload some of the workload that is normally performed by the main CPU. When combined with the strength against physical attack through tamper resistance and tamper evidence, the secure coprocessor offers security functions not easily achieved in a software-only system. It becomes a trusted third party (TTP).

## Attack Vectors

One of the most common secure coprocessors is used in banking and financial transactions (automated teller machines). Its initial release was a FIPS-140 level 4 certified device with tamper resistance. This device provided hardware cryptographic support, random-number generation, and general coprocessor functions. Unfortunately, it had a flaw in its first release of the ATM module that allowed an insider to extract all of the triple DES keys, PIN-derivation algorithms, and importer/exporter keys. Subsequent releases fixed this weakness, but the attack underscores the fact that hardware security is necessary but not sufficient for a secure coprocessor—the algorithms contained within must be designed to thwart attacks that have penetrated the physical barriers of the device.

## Techniques for Creating Strong Coprocessors

The philosophy "cradle to grave security" must be emphasized, implemented, and guarded throughout the development of secure coprocessors. This includes degrees of control (and paranoia) that may seem laughable at times, but such steps raise the cost of attack to levels that divert an attacker to other targets. Such an approach follows the philosophy of home alarm systems—their goal is to make the owner's home sufficiently unattractive that burglars will be diverted to other, less secure homes.

Cradle-to-grave security begins with a secure fabrication facility. Many fabs add debugging pins to facilitate testing of the various modules on the board. A trusted board should have no such "reserved for factory test" or other back-door functions. Use of a secure fab should reduce accidental exposure of functions on the board and should reduce possible attack points.

Coding practices should follow the most rigorous standards and procedures. Several excellent guides to secure software development (such as that written by Howard and Leblanc[1]) contain best practices that should be implemented and enforced by project management. These include, among others, practices such as:

- Creating code in a secure physical environment
- Creation of security modules by employees only (as opposed to outsourcing)
- Extensive and regular code reviews
- Encryption of source code

- Protection of encryption keys
- Logging of access in a remote database

Attacks on a hardware board include a variety of options. Physical inspection of the board can be accomplished with one or more remote-sensing techniques such as the use of x-rays, thermal imaging, and ultrasonic probes. More invasive approaches involve the removal of the case above the actual silicon chip, followed by the use of scanning microscopy or other probing technologies. Although much more costly and labor-intensive, such techniques are not beyond the realm of possibility for systems that are protecting sufficiently valuable information. These more extreme attacks require, where possible, "zeroizing" (erasing) of critical encryption keys and/or data upon sensing of such attacks.

## SECURE BOOTSTRAP LOADING

The term "bootstrap process" (in which a computing system, for example, activates itself from a powered-down situation) has its origins in a legendary story about Baron Munchhausen. In this legend, Munchhausen claimed he was able to lift himself out of a swamp by pulling himself up by his hair. Over time, the legend changed to one in which he lifted himself up by his bootstraps.

In practice, the bootstrap process begins at power-up. The microprocessor always begins executing instructions as a specific memory location in a read-only memory device. This process usually includes a hardware diagnostic test, followed by loading the first sector of a disk (or other storage medium) into memory, and then continues executing the instructions it finds there. It next checks for the presence of an operating system, and then begins executing those instructions. Failure at any point results in notifying the user.

Attacks are mounted by copying the proper boot sector to another portion of the drive and then modifying the memory-resident portion of the operating system. On a subsequent restart, the attack version of the OS is loaded and the normal boot process proceeds to load the attack code.

### Protection of the Bootstrap Process

Unfortunately, one of the compromises made in the design of the low-cost PC was that hardware protection of the operating system, which was standard practice for high-end computers, was discarded. Although rarely used today, the write-protect mechanism that was available on floppy drives and now can be found on flash drives affords a hardware-based protection mechanism for the bootstrap process. If the write-protect mechanism is engaged after a known clean copy of the operating system has been placed on the drive, it effectively disables bootstrap attacks. If boot-protection software is installed on the protected floppy or flash drive, the bootstrap process gains additional protection. So the process would begin by placing the boot block, operating-system files, device drivers, command interpreter, an initialization file, and an integrity-defense program on the floppy or flash drive, and then write-protecting it. The boot sequence of the PC must be altered to include the floppy or flash drive at a higher priority than the hard drive. With these two steps and the use of the floppy or flash drive to boot the PC each time, a user can protect himself against bootstrap attacks. This approach, unfortunately, involves the use of a piece of hardware that can be accidentally left at home (or at the office), thereby preventing the user from achieving a secure bootstrap.

In order to avoid this situation, a piece of hardware can be introduced that is an integral part of the platform (and so cannot be left behind), is initiated at the factory, and includes an inheritance process that establishes progressively higher levels of trust as the contents and versions of hardware and software modules residing on the platform are checked during the bootstrap process. Valid signatures of these modules are stored in secure, encrypted memory on this device at the factory, and the bootstrap process proceeds to check the integrity and validity of modules using these signatures. This process is called "attestation" and is discussed in subsequent chapters.

## SECURE MEMORY MANAGEMENT

Memory management becomes an attack avenue when an attacker creates a buffer overflow, which then allows execution of attack code. This can be accomplished through intentionally exceeding the bounds of allocated memory for arrays and variables and through the use of memory pointers. Memory pointers, as the name implies, are variables or constants that contain the address of code modules or programs that should be executed. Since there are no restrictions on the addresses that can be stored in these pointers, they can point to anything. Hackers either place malicious code at the "indirect addressing" locations or change the pointer to point to malicious code, all without tripping any alarms.

The successful use of these two techniques has gained some degree of publicity in the past year as hackers use them to break widely deployed operating systems, browsers, and other popular applications.

## Protection of Memory Management

The prevention of buffer overflows can be accomplished by adding code that checks to see that writing of data to a buffer (such as a variable, array, or other allocated memory) never exceeds the length allocated to the buffer. Erasing the contents (after use) of buffers that contain critical information (such as encryption keys) is an important associated memory-management practice.

The use of memory pointers should be minimized, and they should be destroyed when they are no longer used. This will at least reduce the threat of memory-pointer attacks.

## TRUSTED PLATFORM MODULE

The Trusted Computing Group (TCG) is an organization with representatives of the leading computer-industry companies worldwide who sought a means to improve computer security and authentication. In particular, the TCG wanted to:

- Create a means for checking system integrity
- Authenticate a system to the network
- Enable secure storage of information

The TCG created the trusted platform module (TPM). The TPM is a chip that creates and securely stores private and public PKI keys and hash values (such as certificates). The TPM chip is tamper-resistant and tamper-evident and resides on the motherboard of a TPM-enabled PC. By separating encryption and decryption keys from a storage medium (such as a hard drive), the removal or theft of a hard drive cannot by itself allow an attacker to decrypt encrypted files without significant effort. Moreover, the TPM can provide initialization and management functions that allow the owner to turn functionality on and off.

As implemented today, the TPM:

- Checks the system integrity and the status of the hardware and software environment
- Authenticates the system to the network
- Enables secure storage, provides hardware-based encryption. And stores keys

- Provides a PC ID, limiting access from unauthorized PCs
- Allows a user to take ownership with strong controls to protect privacy

**TPM Attack Vectors**

Unless a security system removes all passwords from the user and employs its own internal, changing passwords (possibly coupled with a biometric reader of some sort), the dangers of human behavior remain. Users that are required to remember multiple, complex passwords will likely write passwords on a piece of paper and store it in a hidden but easily accessible place. The use of mnemonics to create passwords not only introduces strong keys but reduces the temptation that users might have to write down passwords.

Some implementations of TPM include the creation of a secure kernel and a report of a remote system's integrity. The strength offered by a secure kernel can also be its downfall if a hacker succeeds in installing a virus or worm that can take control of the kernel. Once inside, it can destroy the system's ability to operate and the user's ability to retrieve critical files.

The reporting of system integrity to external parties could possibly be used to provide vital system information. This function should be disabled if possible.

TPM makes extensive use of the secure hash algorithm-1 (SHA-1), a non-reversible cryptographic hash algorithm that provides unique 20-byte "signatures" for any input data stream. SHA-1, supported by NIST[2], is widely used to digitally sign documents or alternatively to provide evidence that a document has not been altered.

In 2005, the cryptographic community was stunned to learn that the SHA-1 algorithm had been broken by three Chinese researchers (Xiaoyun Wang, Yiqun Lisa Yin, and Hongbo Yu at Shandong University). These researchers reduced the amount of time needed to find two documents with the same signature by a factor of more than 2000. As a result, TPM implementations inherit this new weakness, opening a new attack channel.

## LAGRANDE (TRUSTED EXECUTION TECHNOLOGY)

Intel recently launched a secure computing initiative which was code named LaGrande. This technology has been renamed Trusted Execution Technology (TET). TET will be available on Intel's newest-generation microprocessors.

The TET system seeks to close the attack vectors that exist in previous systems using hardware-based security techniques. These attack vectors include:

- Video memory: attack software either captures screen information or creates fake screens to coax the user into revealing security information. Phishing, in which fake web pages or emails are created to coax the user to enter valuable information, is a classic example of this type of attack.

- Input devices: capture software can be installed on a target computer to monitor keyboard and other input activity. Offered as software to "monitor your spouse, kids, or employees," this malware has been remarkably effective in providing passwords and account information to attackers.

- Memory access: an undesirable feature of the DMA architecture is that it allows a peripheral device (such as a PCI card) to directly access system memory without any involvement of the CPU. In this type of attack, the contents of RAM are scoured for valuable information (such as encryption keys or passwords).

## Video Protection

The TET architecture introduces a trusted hardware channel between the software applications and the video card. Employing on-board encryption/decryption capability, this protection will require the replacement of current video cards with TET-enabled cards that include the required encryption/decryption functionality. An alternate approach would require that Intel include integrated graphics on its TET processors.

## Input Devices

The TET system employs hardware encryption and decryption to create trusted channels between the processor and input devices such as a keyboard or mouse. Clearly, TET-compatible keyboards and mice are required in order to enable this feature.

## Memory Protection

Using a technique called domain separation, TET provides protected execution of commands, in which software can be run such that it is isolated from all other software. Using a domain manager, no other software can access an application's data nor control the devices that the application is operating. A table maintains a list of which pages in memory are protected and to which application pages belong. The domain manager blocks access to protected memory pages except by the owning application itself. TET adds domain-specific encryption, in which only software within the designated domain can encrypt or decrypt data. The use of this technique requires the TPM (described above) in addition to a TET-enabled micro-processor and related chipsets.

The TET system employs a feature called "sealed storage" (enabled by TPM) in which data that must be stored for a long time (that is, on a hard drive) must be protected during writing, during storage, and during retrieval. Complete isolation of data by application is an essential part of this feature.

### Trusted Execution Technology Attack Vectors

Most of the features provided by the TET system rely upon the TPM func-tionality described above. As a result, TET will only be as strong as TPM. As a possible weak point, attack vectors for TPM will likely be employed by an attacker to gain complete access to a TET-protected system. Proper attention must be paid to the installation and maintenance of the TPM sys-tem in order to reap its benefits. Nonetheless, since the TET system relies extensively on TPM and TPM makes wide use of the now broken SHA-1 algorithm, TET deployments that use SHA-1 inherit the recently discov-ered attack vectors that are imbedded in TPM.

The use of global encryption keys (which are attractive to administra-tors since they add a degree of uniformity to protected systems and sim-plify maintenance) must be avoided in order to prevent a single attack from possibly yielding complete access to a multiplicity of systems and their resources.

## FIELD-PROGRAMMABLE GATE ARRAY

An FPGA is a device that offers programmable logic components and pro-grammable interconnects between the logic components. FPGAs are often used to create systems on a chip (SOC). SOCs offer the advantage that all components of the embedded system are on a single chip die. With the proper security features, such SOCs can offload processing tasks from the main processor and provide self-contained security functions that can be protected by the physical construction of the chip. The FPGA technology provides a natural platform for SOC implementations, but several factors need to be considered during the design phase of any secure processor based on an FPGA.

The selected device must have the following security features:

- On-board encryption
- Encrypted programmable read-only memory
- "Zeroize" capability for key destruction
- Secure key storage, inaccessible to the outside world once the device has been programmed
- Secure design practices during development to protect the design and keys

It is critical that proper attention be paid to several components of the FPGA during the design process. FPGAs, like any other device, have input/output (IO) pins. An attacker will likely begin his attacks by examining the IO pins for possible vulnerabilities or paths into sensitive areas of the module. Direct as well as indirect (coupling) paths to sensitive information must be addressed during the design phase.

Debugging is an important capability for any computer technology, since bug-free designs are virtually impossible. Nonetheless, debug access can also be used by a knowledgeable attacker to gain access to or information about critical modules within an FPGA. Design of a secure debug architecture is critical to the ultimate security of the device.

The FPGA architecture itself should be subjected to multiple, independent design reviews by trusted individuals before commitment to a design becomes too expensive to reverse. Security errors in the architecture design must be eliminated up front rather than through application of patches later.

The design software itself must be selected based on its ability to support the development of a secure FPGA design. Access to the design software and the designs themselves must be carefully controlled and granted only to those key design-team members with a need to know. Policies must be enacted to protect the designs during storage or transport within or outside the development environment.

The design of the board layout should include a review by an independent electronics engineer for possible security risks associated with shielding of signals. Power supply traces should be examined for possible presence of signals (due to power demands) that might reveal critical information.

The design/layout/architecture diagrams of an FPGA implementation are valuable not only as intellectual property but also as roadmaps to possible vulnerabilities within the design. Storage of such designs offline (without any Internet connections) should be further protected by the use of encryption, limited and recorded access, change-control software, and physical protection.

Many designs today use open-source software or architecture concepts as a means to leverage otherwise costly development time and dollars. Since such external software was not necessarily subjected to the same security reviews that should be applied to internally developed designs, it needs to be evaluated for possible introduction of security vulnerabilities.

Optimization software can eliminate inefficiencies in the design of an FPGA, but its use should require an additional security review after optimization to assure that no security features that were designed into the FPGA were removed by the optimization tool.

## HARDWARE-BASED AUTHENTICATION

The authentication of parties over the Internet (or any other remote communication protocol) can be classified into one of two categories:

- Technologies that authenticate the person
- Technologies that authenticate the device upon which he is operating

We will introduce the technologies at a high level in this chapter and examine each in more detail in later chapters.

### Person Authentication Using Biometrics

In order to authenticate that a person sitting at the other end of a communication channel is indeed who he claims to be, something must authenticate the person. Some systems employ a simple PIN or password, trusting the user to keep it secret. This is commonly referred to as "something you know." As the reader can appreciate, human nature often causes the user to write the password down, often in an insecure manner, and often in a hidden but easy-to-access location (such as under the keyboard or the mouse pad). For this reason, software-based authentication systems should be avoided in favor of hardware-based systems.

Hardware-based authentication systems employ a device of some sort with which the user must interact in order to authenticate his identity.

(This type of authentication is referred to in some circles as "something you are.") The device usually employs a measurement that is user-specific (such as a fingerprint, for example) and that has been demonstrated to be sufficiently unique that the probability of finding a duplicate is vanishingly low. Examples of common hardware-based person-authentication technologies are introduced below.

*Fingerprint Scanners*
It has long been asserted that each person's fingerprint is unique. A recent mathematical study of this claim has allowed the quantification of the probability of finding two people with the same fingerprint, and this study largely confirms that such an event is unlikely. In a seminal paper by Osterburg et al.[3], it was shown that, for a system that measures 12 of the most common fingerprint characteristics, the probability of finding a match is less than $10^{-20}$. Reduction of the number of characteristics measured increases this probability, but most fingerprint readers operate with 12 measurements or more.

The uniqueness notwithstanding, a person's fingerprint as measured by a device produces a unique digital signature. In order for fingerprints to be useful, they must be unchanging. Therefore, this unique digital signature is static, and as a static identifier, it must be stored in some fashion in order to be recognized at a later date. The static nature of the fingerprint, coupled with the need to store this digitally, creates an attack point for the system. In principle, an attacker who has obtained the stored signature could feed this signature in to the challenge/response portion of the authentication system and thereby obtain "recognition." Although the difficulty of such an interception/replacement step should not be minimized, the static nature of the fingerprint remains an attack point. By the same token, an attack on the fingerprint database and replacement of a target fingerprint with the attacker's fingerprint could also succeed if the database has not been sufficiently protected.

Fingerprint biometric devices will be discussed in greater detail in a subsequent chapter of this book.

*Voiceprints*
In a manner similar to the fingerprint technology described above, voiceprints employ stable vocal characteristics to establish a uniqueness upon which a person's authentication can subsequently be determined. Since stress and physical health can affect a person's voice, the voiceprint technology has been developed around a set of measurements that are unique for each person but insensitive to variable conditions. The stable charac-

teristics express the physical configuration of a person's mouth and throat as a mathematical formula for a voice sample that was recorded in a trusted environment. Specific words may be recorded during the enrollment process. This enables the software to request words in a random sequence, thereby reducing the likelihood of a digital recording of the person being used to defeat the system. Authentication of a person using a voiceprint employs the samples recorded during enrollment, the derived mathematical formula based on those recordings, and a mathematical analysis of the vocal sample being presented.

Like fingerprint biometric devices, the voiceprint is a static identifier (in this case, the mathematical analysis/representation of a user's voiceprint). Although the use of random shuffling of requested test words reduces the possibility of recording a digital voice to overcome the system, the number of separate words and the combinations thereof might represent the weakest link in the security of the voiceprint system, since digital recordings of voices represent high-fidelity recordings that could be captured by other means. As with the fingerprint technology, an attack in which the algorithm is replaced by one that matches the attacker's voice might also prove to be an approachable attack channel.

### *Iris Scans*

Similar to fingerprint and voiceprint recognition technologies, iris scans analyze unique and stable features in the iris of a person's eye. Most iris scans employ more than 200 measurement points as the basis for comparison. Features such as rings, furrows, spots, and color distribution provide the basis for recognition. Some implementations require the presence of pupil response in order to discriminate between live data and an image of the target's iris. Iris scans offer some advantages over technologies such as retinal scans, since the former do not require the proximity and low light levels required of the latter.

This authentication technology shares the same attack issues as fingerprint and voiceprint technologies. The static identifier (the collection of 200 measured points) could be captured and fed into the software to bypass the device. An attacker's iris scan could replace a target user's iris scan.

### *Palm Prints*

Much like the fingerprint technology described above, palm prints utilize unique and stable characteristics present on the human palm to create an identifier. The larger size of the palm-print reader is thought to have contributed to its slower adoption in spite of its (superior) abundance of unique characteristics.

Attack avenues for palm-print readers match those of the fingerprint readers and will not be repeated here.

## Radio-Frequency IDs

In addition to the authentication approaches described above ("something you know" and "something you are"), there is a class of authentication technologies collectively referred to as "something you have," In this class of tokens, the user must carry a unique device, which is then used to demonstrate his identity (assuming that the user has not lost his token). One such token is the RFID.

Typically, the RFID is a flat card or other small token that is easily carried by a user. The unit carries miniature electronic circuitry that responds to a specific sequence of signals received at a specific frequency and "reports back" by transmitting a set of identifiers (possibly encrypted) in response. The unit that performs the radio-frequency query then submits the received information to an algorithm that determines whether or not the user's RFID response matches what was expected. This algorithm might simply use the RFID to determine the identity of the user and log his entry to a building, or it might perform a more complex action. Depending on the specific RFID frequency and the strength of the query unit's transmission system, this technology can operate anywhere from a proximity range (inches) to many feet.

## Hardware Based RNGs

In addition to their possible role as a source of nonpredictable keys, hardware-based random number generators can also be employed as part of an authentication system. Such a system usually involves a challenge/response process in which one party presents a question (referred to as the "challenge") and the other party (the user) responds with the answer (the "response"). The use of RNGs in this role requires that an initial pair of RNG-generated challenge/response values be issued to both parties at the time of enrollment. If these response values do not change, the system becomes progressively more susceptible to eavesdropping attacks with each successive transmission of the challenge and the response. An alternative is to make the challenge/response pair dynamic, changing the response values each time. This implementation requires that the new response value be shared securely between the two parties. Some implementations use a session-based key to achieve a secure transmission of the new challenge/response pair. The use of dynamic response values in a challenge/response process is more secure than the use of static pairs, but security of the system hinges on the strength of the session key used to transmit the updated response.

The use of a hardware-based RNG is preferable to PRGs, as explained in a previous chapter.

## Hardware Token Authenticators

An alternate technology that employs the "something you have" philosophy of authentication involves the use of a small token that generates a code at fixed intervals of time. Initialized with a PRG "seed" at the factory, such a token is unique to each user. When employed as part of a challenge/response system, the user is typically challenged to enter his PIN ("something you know") as well as the number currently being displayed on the token ("something you have"). The combination of the two is hashed and compared to the response expected for this user with his personal token at this particular moment in time. (The server "knows" the time and can predict, based on the knowledge of this user's seed, what his token should be displaying.) Combined with the PIN, this creates a two-factor authentication process that is enjoying widespread use at this time. Proper implementations use tamper-resistant designs, and some also include a "duress code," a special PIN to be used only to alert the server that the user was forced to enter his PIN.

It is important to note that two-factor authentication is not used to encrypt information—the encryption function is provided by the protocol layer (SSL, VPN, etc.). Moreover, protection of the PIN from acquisition by anyone else is a critical responsibility of a user in protecting access to the remote system.

Attack vectors for this technology can employ phishing-type screens in which the user is tricked into entering his PIN and token number—this could be used by an attacker to immediately establish a connection to the server (a "man in the middle" attack), thereby preventing the legitimate user from logging in. Once logged in, the attacker could then gain access to protected information and possibly to the authentic user's credential information as well.

In the following chapters, the key technologies described above will be examined in more depth so that the reader can establish a more thorough understanding of the various hardware approaches. This knowledge should enable the reader to begin to define a set of hardware-based security technologies that are best suited for a specific environment.

## REFERENCES

[1] Howard, Michael and LeBlanc, David, *Writing Secure Code*, 2nd ed., Redmond, WA, Microsoft Press, 2003. (ISBN 0735617228)

[2] "The Secure Hash Algorithm (SHA-1)," National Institute of Standards and Technology, NIST FIPS PUB 180–1, *"Secure Hash Standard,"* U.S. Department of Commerce, April 1995.

[3] J.Osterburg, et al., "Development of a Mathematical Formula for the Calculation of Fingerprint Probabilities Based on Individual Characteristics," *Journal of the American Statistical Association*, Vol. 72, No. 360, 1977, pp. 772–778, 1977.

# Chapter 5

## SECURE COPROCESSORS

### THE NEED FOR SECURE COPROCESSORS

As explained in the overview of secure coprocessors in Chapter 4, the primary motivation for using a secure coprocessor is to create a protected environment, separate from the operating system's CPU, in which applications requiring high security can operate. Not only does this approach allow the use of hardware-based encryption, encapsulated keys, and the protection of data and program information from external observation or interference, but it also relieves some of the demand for computing cycles that would otherwise be placed on the host system's CPU. Moreover, such a secure coprocessor must be able to authenticate the applications that it is using and authenticate itself to the outside world. It must operate with the additional constraint that the only time that the coprocessor is in a completely known state and environment is at the time of manufacture. It must employ a trust-inheritance process that builds upon the initial conditions and adds authentication information about the user, the applications that it is using, and the platform on which it is operating.

A secure coprocessor is a separate physical device, so applications that operate external to it must be able to authenticate any data or results obtained from the coprocessor, thereby assuring that the results have not been tampered with as they travel from the coprocessor back out to the external environment. Moreover, the administrator must be able to interact with the secure coprocessor in order to maintain configuration information and provide any additional required updates or service, and he must be able to do so in an unprotected environment.

Some implementations of secure-coprocessor technologies might involve the creation of small, secure, portable devices that offer a heightened degree of trust and protection when compared to conventional computer platforms. Portability offers enhanced ease of use, and, if properly configured, allows the use of otherwise untrusted host platforms for sensitive transactions. Other implementations of secure coprocessor technology embed the separate device on the host platform in a nonportable way.

Design of a secure coprocessor is all about risk minimization and designer paranoia. Designers have to assume that errors will occur during installation, updating, and operation of the coprocessor or that an attacker will induce those errors intentionally. Designers must think like an attacker, anticipating as broadly as possible any attacks that might occur as a result of induced errors or other compromises in the system integrity.

## PHYSICAL SECURITY

In order to provide a secure environment in which applications and their associated data can operate, it is essential that the secure coprocessor be protected against physical attacks. To date, no one has proven that "tamperproof" can be achieved, so most work in recent years has focused on tamper resistance. Tamper resistance requires the inclusion of tamper-detection circuits that not only display nonreversible evidence of tampering to the user but also protect the contents of the card by erasing ("zeroizing") any cryptographic keys and other secret information.

The most difficult area of tamper-resistance technology focuses on penetration techniques. Detection of known penetration techniques is a prerequisite for deciding when to activate tamper-protection circuitry. Design approaches must be based on penetration studies[1]. Penetration approaches include techniques such as externally induced failures, manipulation of the external environment (temperature, voltage levels, ionizing radiation, RF noise, etc.), and advanced scanning to read data.

Sensors for all conceivable attacks should be included (where the price of these sensors is justified by the value of the information that is being protected). For example, "tamper-aware" circuitry might include the presence of layers of wire grids whose impedance characteristics are continually monitored for changes. These layers can be "potted" or otherwise attached irreversibly to the circuitry that they are protecting so that physical probing can trigger zeroizing. Of course, the use of electromagnetic shields to minimize RF penetration is also encouraged.

Sensing and zeroizing circuitry both require power, so reliance on externally supplied power is not adequate to allow continual protection of the secure coprocessor. Battery supplies must be built into the innermost, protected portions of the circuitry so that any physical attempt to disconnect the battery is sensed and zeroizing action is taken before such a disconnection can occur. Certain types of storage elements can develop a residual image of the protected data over sufficiently long storage times, so periodic inversion or bit address rotations should be included to avoid possible post attack detection of keys. Clock attacks, in which the host clock timing is altered to cause a failure in a depended-upon coprocessor, can be avoided by using clocks that are internal to the coprocessor.

## INITIALIZATION

A secure coprocessor that has just exited the manufacturing line has no content in application, cryptography, or cryptographic-key sections of its memory. The process of initializing the coprocessor establishes this initial condition from which all subsequent authentications will be checked. As explained in Chapter 1 of this book, asymmetric key cryptography is generally a stronger encryption, especially if the keys have their origins in a hardware-based key generator. Ideally, the coprocessor uses a hardware-based RNG to generate the public/private key pair internally, stores the private key in secure memory on board, and then provides the public key to the administrator who is initializing the board. The distribution and storage of the public key can then be controlled by organizational policy or by employing certifying authorities for redundant backup. The administrator can then create a digital hash, which is generated by the initialization parameters of the card, with the hash then stored both internally in secure memory and externally on the administrator's database.

Initialization forms the foundation upon which future issuing of new keys by the coprocessor is based. Once a trusted coprocessor has been created in this fashion, its current private key can be used to encrypt and/or sign the new public key as well as digitally sign any new configuration changes that might occur as a result of new key generation. The combination of cradle-to-grave trust with frequent changes to the keys (to avoid static attack points) creates a secure environment for the subsequent use of the coprocessor. To the extent that a certifying authority is employed for holding keys, this process also accommodates updating of CA certificates.

A critical part of the initialization process (and subsequently the upgrade process) is the safe loading of code into the coprocessor. The designer must consider a variety of security issues related to loading of code into the secure coprocessor:

- How will the existing (loaded) code authenticate updated code?
- How is the memory location into which the new code is being installed guaranteed?
- How is the updating of lower modules upon which the target module depends handled?
- What assures that the code that checks signatures is authentic?

Successful resolution of these issues hinges on the design and implementation of the authentication protocols (discussed below).

## USABILITY, ACCESSIBILITY, AND SECURITY

The need for ease of use, access to secure information, and the protection thereof often leads to conflicts in requirements. Ultimately the designer must balance the three competing demands and decide on an implementation that offers a reasonable compromise to the security-minded customer. There is no formula for determining the balance point—it must be reached by the developer. However, it is best if the developer keep the following in mind when trying to reach that balance.

The demand for "ease of use" often includes the desire for the simplest possible administrative authentication process. Unfortunately, such processes often rely upon less than secure authentication supported, for example, by the host operating system. Since the strength of a system's security is determined by its weakest point, the desire for "ease of use" can lead to reduced security of the secure coprocessor unit. The developer needs to approach this request with heightened awareness of possible weaknesses that might be introduced by employing existing system-authentication mechanisms.

Usability also places demands on basic tools and architecture of the secure coprocessor. Customers typically desire that common operating systems and associated debugging tools be present on the coprocessor in order to minimize the need for new sets of skills. The coprocessor must generally be designed to allow the operation and isolation of multiple authorized developers, each of whom might seek access to specific portions of the coprocessor. Isolation must be complete, with no access by a user who is authorized to access one vertical component to any other vertical components.

Accessibility is another capability that tends to run counter to good security practices. For example, as explained in Chapter 4, it is best if the secure coprocessor has tamper-resistant packaging, preferably with automatic zeroizing of cryptographic keys in the event of a physical breach. However, the author has experienced a situation in which, following zeroizing of cryptographic keys, the customer requested that the system (or the administrator) restore the keys that have been erased in order to provide accessibility to information that is being protected by the zeroizing event. Of course, this request raises the question as to where copies of the cryptographic keys reside that allow such a restoration. How are those copies of keys protected? How is the administrator who performs the restoration authenticated, and what measures are taken to prevent an attacker from using this process to either gain access or introduce compromised keys into the card? The questions spiral onward, ultimately without a satisfactory conclusion. The author recommends against the use of "revival" techniques as fundamentally nonsecure.

Security is the ultimate purpose of the existence of a secure coprocessor. Therefore, all measures should be taken to protect the security of the device and the data and applications that it stores. It is the author's opinion that ease of use and accessibility requests by the customer take lower priority to maintaining the security of the system, even if these requests ultimately have to be denied.

Careful attention must be paid to the data paths between the secure coprocessor and the outside, untrusted world. Designs should assume that data entering the device must be treated as suspect. Functions of convenience, such as infrared or RF data links for ease of use, can introduce attack paths. Hackers can not only flood such pathways with data to try to immobilize a targeted device but also can use these paths for eavesdropping and capture of data packets.

## SUPPORT AND UPGRADES

Secure coprocessors, like any other device that hosts a CPU and various other security modules, will require the application of upgrades, bug fixes, and patches from time to time. Such upgrades need to be enabled (with proper authentication of the administrator and the incoming code) for all elements of the coprocessor, including its operating system, cryptographic modules, and digital signing algorithms.

Careful attention must be paid to the authentication required by an administrator before such a patch can be applied in order to minimize possible associated security risks. It should be designed such that, even if the current software on the coprocessor is entirely nonfunctioning (due to serious bugs or even the crippling of the device due to an attack), an upgrade or other patch can still be applied.

Applications of patches or upgrades should not stop the operation of the device or at least should minimize the time required to complete the upgrade. Remote application of upgrades should be tolerated if sufficient security measures are in place to prevent unauthorized access with the same or more security than is provided by the coprocessor itself.

## ANTICIPATORY DESIGN

Careful planning is an essential part of any project, but its importance is dramatically elevated when designing a product such as a secure coprocessor. It is important that the design team attempt to anticipate potential attacks and consider the possibility that the security of the device has been compromised at all possible levels. Doing so reduces the risk of (unpleasant!) surprises and the need for recalls and urgent redesigns.

In principle, the secure coprocessor will run secure applications within its environment after confirming that the application is authentic, that its input and output can be trusted, and that the person requesting the operation has also been authenticated. Designers need to consider the following possible conditions and design the security of the system to prevent operation of subverted code. As a worst case, assume that:

- The secure application has been replaced with a subverted version
- The OS within the secure coprocessor has been replaced with a compromised version either before or after installation of the secure application

- The cryptographic module and/or its keys have been replaced with compromised versions (perhaps with back doors)

## AUTHENTICATION

One of the keys to accomplishing protection against the above attack scenarios is to employ strong authentication among the elements of the secure coprocessor and between the coprocessor and the outside world. The topic of authentication has been covered at a high level in Chapters 1 and 4 and will be covered in greater detail in a later chapter. Nonetheless, authentication is a critical element of a properly deployed secure processor.

Creation of a secure processing environment for applications and their data requires that an authentic coprocessor be distinguishable from a compromised device during periodic audits of the system security. This requires authentication of the device and its software by an administrator or remote processing elements.

Where practical, the most trusted administrator authentication of the secure coprocessor will occur when the coprocessor is in the direct physical presence of the administrator. This allows an expert to perform an examination of the card for any evidence of physical tampering and avoids transmission of any authentication or configuration information over remote networks.

The physical presence of such an administrator is not always practical, however, so the coprocessor must be enabled to provide proper authentication information to a remote administrator in a manner that minimizes security exposure.

One implementation of authentication protocols assigns authorities to successively higher levels of applications. For example, the root authority is the sole authority that can control updates and installations of the boot code and core encryption (and authentication) services. Above this (at higher functionality but lower authority) are those authorities that "own" individual operating systems. Above these would appear authorities for individual applications that run on top of the operating systems. In true hierarchical fashion, higher authorities dominate those that have lower privileges. Of course, isolation of the authorities and their privileges is critical. Private and public keys for each authority reside in nonvolatile memory for that authority's code segment. The device and its applications should authenticate messages using its private and public key pairs for its communication with other modules or the outside world.

This dual-key approach suffers from a potential problem when performing outbound authentication. In particular, in the event that an application that is being employed has changed due to the application of a patch or upgrade, the public key that authenticates its use will change. It is quite likely that the receiving (remote) party requesting authentication may not recognize the patch as valid. In fact, this concern raises the question of how outbound authentication by secure coprocessors differentiates between trusted and malicious patches to code modules. A mechanism must be developed that allows a remote entity to recognize the use of an application that has had legitimate software patches applied from a maliciously altered application. This must be addressed by developers in order for secure coprocessor technology to propagate widely.

Creation of such a stratified, hierarchical structure, each element with its own asymmetric key pair, enables the digital signing of data, code-configuration information, or other results with each element separate from all others. If the elements are carefully stratified and separated in hardware, key pairs can not only be hardware-protected and element-specific but can also enable graceful separation of authentication tasks regarding upgrades of separate elements at different times.

The designers need to be cognizant of the fact that a sufficiently funded attacker can either create a duplicate or modify a secure processor device that will not be distinguishable from a card that has not been altered. All that remains to allow a user to distinguish between real and altered is the use of hardware-protected key pairs within the individual elements. If the keys have been created using a proper cradle-to-grave loading and upgrade authentication process as described above, with a fully authenticated administrator on site at the point of shipment, external controls (such as biometrics and physical access) using systems independent of and complementary to the secure coprocessor issuing system should ensure that a card can only be initialized by an original, trusted administrator. To the extent that remote initialization of the card by an administrator is enabled or allowed, risk of attack will be raised accordingly. Depending on the value of information being stored or processed on the card, the choices regarding remote initialization should be deliberated fully before a decision is taken.

All applications, with the exception of the controlled-access initialization tool controlled by the authorized manufacturing administrator, must not be granted access to any of the system-critical secrets, such as the initialization keys. Strict enforcement of memory partitioning by the hardware will go a long way towards assuring this protection. Physical protection of the device administrator's loading protocol software is also essential to this security.

To the extent that system initialization keys have been installed securely at the point of shipping by access-controlled software and by an administrator who has been authenticated by independent means, the device can be securely reset or otherwise remotely managed. The tamper-resistant/evident hardware should provide the zeroizing of these initialization keys, so an altered device will not be able to respond correctly to a challenge/response process that would be initiated at the start of such a remote executive operation.

To the extent that secure coprocessors are used as an element of the authentication process of a user ("something you have"), the technology offers additional protection due to the difficulty of producing a copy or fake token. Secure coprocessor authentication tokens can be strengthened by introducing a challenge/response process in which the token and/or the user must interact in the process to complete the authentication. Further enhancement can be achieved by introducing changing elements within the challenge-response process. These might be event-driven (a table of secrets changes with each authentication) or time-driven (for example, contents change once every five minutes). These elements can reduce the risk of attack by data capture, since the answers to a challenge change each time, preferably in unpredictable ways.

None of these approaches can eliminate the threat of a malicious user. However, the technology does provide an option for audit trails. Although not as appealing as protection, it does provide subsequent recourse should such a user perform such an action.

## REFERENCES

[1] D. Chaum (Ed.), "Design Concepts for Tamper-Responding Systems," D. Chaum, Advances in Cryptology Proceedings of Crypto 83, Plenum, pp. 387–392.

# Chapter 6

## SECURE BOOTSTRAP LOADING

### THE NEED FOR SECURE BOOTSTRAP LOADING

Over the years, attacks on computing systems, intent on gaining access to personal or other valuable information, have included a variety of viruses and Trojan-horse applications that attack the operating system during the bootstrap process. As the use of the Internet and email has exploded in recent years, the ease with which such attacks can be propagated has increased dramatically. These attacks, coupled with various others described elsewhere in this book, have resulted in the loss of untold billions of dollars of valuable information and have caused great personal distress for individuals whose identity has been stolen. Protection against bootstrap-loading attacks, in which the bootstrap process is replaced with a compromised bootstrap that loads an infected operating system, is an essential part of the solution. The bootstrap process was introduced in Chapter 4.

In order to alleviate the demand on the CPU, many devices have built-in processors that operate autonomously—disk controllers, coprocessors, network cards, and more. Since each of these devices contains processing elements that could be replaced by compromised and infected firmware, it is important that the bootstrap process of a computer not only include the verification of the main host CPU elements but also any and all firmware-driven devices that are attached to the computer at boot-up time.

## IMPLEMENTATION

Security, authenticity, and trust begin at the most primitive level and propagate to progressively higher and higher levels of dependent code. The introduction of a compromise anywhere in the chain of trust eliminates trustworthiness from that point forward.

The first step in this inheritance begins with the bootstrap process. Arbaugh, Farber, and Smith[1] describe the essentials of a secure inheritance-based trust model that begins with the bootstrap. In their design, the integrity of each step of the bootstrap process is validated with digital signatures that were created using asymmetric cryptography in a secure and trusted environment back at the code origin. This approach, of course, requires that the signatures be checked by some processor, most likely the CPU. The first firmware component to run is the BIOS, or basic input-output system. This is typically stored in some form of rewriteable storage, since the BIOS must be updated to accommodate bug fixes. As such, an obvious attack avenue for this sort of implementation would be the compromise of the bootstrap process, its digital signatures (if not stored in ROM), and the BIOS that must authenticate them. Clearly, storing the digital signatures in ROM does not ultimately provide sufficient protection against such an attack if both the BIOS and the bootstrap can be altered.

The Trusted Computing Group[2] has supported the use of a secure hardware device that can independently verify the BIOS and its verification. This allows remote verification that the operating system began with the computer in a trustworthy state. The trusted platform module[3] (TPM) is an example of such a hardware device. In operation, the TPM employs hashing to create state signatures of code modules. During secure initialization, the TPM creates and stores a small code segment, the core root of trust for measurement (CRTM) in secure storage called the platform configuration register (PCR). Whenever the computer is reset, the CRTM is run first. The CRTM measures all executable firmware (including the

BIOS) against the hash codes that were stored in the PCR during secure initialization. If successful, control is then transferred to the BIOS (which is now trusted), and the BIOS repeats the hash verification process for the initial program loader. The trusted IPL then measures code that it will load, and the process continues in this fashion through the remaining modules, such as the kernel, device drivers, and applications.

A visual flow chart of the TPM bootstrap process is shown in Figure 6.1.

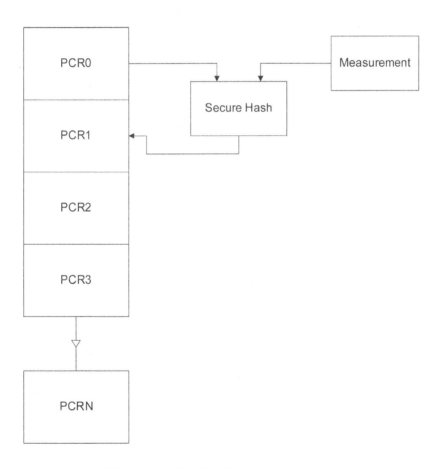

**Figure 6.1** The TPM bootstrap process.

The process reflects the inheritance procedure that begins with the root and consecutively adds signatures for subsequent hardware and software modules whose integrity and trust are required in order to create a trusted computing environment.

At this point, a remote administrator can issue a request to the TPM device, asking for the signatures of each module that is stored in the PCR. This enables the administrator to verify that the system was loaded correctly and can be trusted. The TPM itself cannot be verified, but, as hardware, it is more difficult to attack. Thus the degree of difficulty in attacking such a system has been raised. However, probing of the TPM is not detected, nor is the replacement of the TPM with compromised hardware that can subvert the authentication process. This is sometimes referred to as a remote attestation challenge or, more simply, attestation. Its purpose is to supply the net result of the attestation and trust-inheritance process to a remote system that seeks to ascribe a level of trust to the platform in question. The attestation process should not compromise user privacy in any way or include the transmission of personal user information.

## HARDWARE, FIRMWARE, AND SOFTWARE

In general it is better to trust hardware than to trust either firmware or software. Properly designed hardware can include tamper-evidence or tamper-protection capabilities, and the cost of creating a fake hardware device without the tamper protection included (or, alternatively, disabled) is quite high and often requires significant facilities and technical skill. Firmware and software, in contrast, are easily distributed, making them a much easier target for someone intent on compromising the bootstrap process. In fact, viruses and Trojan horses can be created that target exactly these firmware and software modules.

As with other security technologies, the human element often provides the easiest avenue for an attack. People can be compromised, bribed, tricked, or threatened. The use of such tactics could easily result in a target hard drive with valuable information being "loaned" to the attacker for a short period of time. During this period, an attacker could steal copies of sensitive data, plant system-level viruses, or add a "sleeper" function that is instantiated after a certain calendar date. Upon instantiation, the sleeper code could cause the disk to appear to malfunction, thereby causing the owner to send it in for additional or repeat service. Of course, the attacker knows the date on which this will occur and can arrange to conveniently appear at the compromised technician's workplace for another brief "loan."

The ultimate goal of a hardware attack is to obtain valuable data. Short of obtaining a target hardware device as described above, the next attack path would likely focus on the firmware. Unlike higher-level software, firmware is not overwritten by reinstalling software. It often requires a special-purpose software routine that "burns" the firmware into the device, a process rarely used by a typical user. However, it is not beyond the capability of an intent attacker. Like an operating system, firmware can be compromised. Nonetheless, an administrator should not assume that firmware can be trusted because it is harder to attack—history has shown that as users create security solutions that prevent one type of attack, attackers develop new solutions that sidestep the new protection. This will apply to firmware as well as to operating systems and applications.

There are several ways to launch an attack on firmware that can ultimately compromise an entire system. The most direct way is to provide a targeted user with the firmware update and the required "burning" code and convince him that he should install the update.

A less direct way, although ultimately far more pervasive, is to insert an attacker in the device delivery process. This is likely to be a person or compromised firm that receives the hardware from the manufacturer and is responsible for either installing software or otherwise preparing and delivering the target device to the end user. During the period when the targeted devices are in the possession of the attacker or his firm, compromised firmware can be burned into the device before shipping.

An attack can occur closer to the user. For example, a company that provides software installation and configuration services could install compromised firmware. Maintenance crews can perform a similar function when devices are delivered to them for handling.

Once an attacker has succeeded in installing compromised firmware, the user and system data will likely become available to the attacker in short order. Some devices can issue direct memory access (DMA) commands that allow it to read or write data present in memory, including sensitive data. Devices that are running compromised firmware can certainly deliver data that it is receiving to other locations over the network to which the computer is attached or, alternatively, store the data in a secret location that can be retrieved when the device is either later connected to the network or sent in for service.

## THE TRUSTED COMPUTING BASE

To the extent possible, devices and their firmware should be included in the trusted computing base (TCB). The presence of a device in this base signifies that it has been authenticated at a trusted source (preferably at the manufacturing location), thereby conferring inheritance of trust to subsequent modules as described above.

It is instructive to digress at this point to comment on some of the features present in the common-criteria (CC) process that have bearing on the inclusion of hardware and firmware in the TCB. Common criteria is an ISO/IEC standard for computer security. It is an assurance standard in which users can specify their computer-security requirements and vendors can use this information in the development of their products. It has developed a framework in which vendors can map functions within their products to certain functions required by users (these become the claims). Independent testing labs can then use the CC framework to test the product against the claims using this framework and assign a numerical grade to the product based on the results. The protection levels that can be achieved by products are graded from evaluation-assurance level (EAL) 1 through EAL 7, with higher numbers reflecting more demands upon the development of the security functions.

CC includes an auditing process that seeks to confirm that developers have achieved a certain level of security in the design and implementation of their product. This auditing process involves the careful examination of the company's security target (ST) by an independent group of security auditors in order to confirm that the target of evaluation (TOE) is adequately protected. (The TOE is the actual product that is being protected.) The ST essentially describes the security properties of the TOE by revealing the steps taken by the company to create the TOE.

In order to achieve a claimed level of security, the ST must demonstrate that certain security functional requirements (SFRs), individual security functions provided by the product, have been implemented in a secure manner. The process of auditing the SFRs (such as, for example, how an administrator might authenticate himself to the product's administration function modules) reveals interdependencies among them and can expose security risks that might not have been anticipated by the design team.

In anticipation of a subsequent audit and certification by the CC process, companies must make clear architectural decisions about which system components (hardware, firmware, and software) will reside within the boundary of the TOE and which will not. This process, and the subsequent auditing of module security and interdependence, would be a valuable addition to the development of secure and trusted components in the bootstrap process. By using such an organized procedure to determine the boundaries of the TCB (much like the boundaries of the TOE), developers are much less likely to inadvertently create systems with major attack points. Clearly, any hardware, firmware, or software element that is not included within the boundary of the TCB is automatically flagged as unsafe and can be treated accordingly by higher-level code.

## CONCLUDING REMARKS

The creation of a secure bootstrap process requires the establishment of trust and attestation at the manufacturing source, followed by the inheritance of that trust to any hardware, firmware, and bootstrap-critical software that has been designed to reside within the protected environment (the TCB). This creates a tree of trust whose origins are at the most elemental components of the bootstrap process, and the validation of those elements should be available through independent means from the manufacturer through a digital certificate. Attestation must also enable remote systems to challenge the trustworthiness of a platform.

Attention must be paid to dependencies of the components. Even if a component has been established as trusted, if it relies upon a separate element whose validity cannot be established, then the component can no longer be trusted and should be flagged as such. Higher-level functions should seek to establish the trustworthiness of each lower-level device and act accordingly—those devices that cannot be trusted should be constrained to gain access only to memory areas that are not secure or trusted, for example.

### The Benefits of Secure Bootstrapping

The proper development and implementation of a secure bootstrap process, including the establishment of trust at the point of manufacturing and the subsequent creation of inheritance trees within the TCB, reduces attack points to hardware only. (Attacks on any firmware and software components within the TCB would be detectable by the presence of an improper signature or invalid hash within the PCR.) Hardware attacks can be protected to some extent by using tamper-evident technologies that erase security-related information upon physical attack.

Secure bootstrapping provides the administrator with the ability to remotely detect attacks by checking hash signatures of the components. Patches to code can be verified through use of the trust-inheritance structure of the system, thereby providing an upgrade path that can be trusted.

By limiting access of untrusted modules to nonsecure memory addresses only, the potential for buffer overflow attacks and unauthorized access to encryption keys can be nearly eliminated. In the hardware domain, tamper evidence can be implemented to provide protection of sensitive information.

Implementation of secure bootstrapping provides the platform on which trust can be built, ultimately producing a more secure system and computing environment.

## REFERENCES

[1] W. A. Arbaugh, D. J. Farber, and J. M. Smith, "A secure and reliable bootstrap architecture," Proceedings of the 1997 *IEEE Symposium on Security and Privacy*, May 1997, pp. 65–71, May 1997.

[2] The Trusted Computing Group, http://www.trustedcomputinggroup.org.

[3] The Trusted Computing Group, TPM Main: Part 1 Design Principles, October 2003.

# Chapter 7

## SECURE MEMORY MANAGEMENT AND TRUSTED EXECUTION TECHNOLOGY

In this chapter we discuss two separate but somewhat related topics—secure memory management and Intel's trusted execution technology (formerly called LaGrande).

### THE NEED FOR SECURE MEMORY MANAGEMENT

Secure memory management became an item of increased attention when buffer overflows were used to gain access to secure information or otherwise compromise the security of a system or application. Moreover, it became apparent that poor memory-management techniques by developers were leaving encryption keys and passwords in volatile memory after use, creating additional paths for attacks.

Two technology factors have also contributed to the increased need for secure memory management. First, the increase of multitasking has increased the importance of proper isolation of memory between applications. Second, the use of the Internet to propagate viruses and Trojan-horse programs provided an easy attack path that could be exploited at arbitrary distances and at any time of day or night.

In this chapter, we examine the nature of memory-management attack paths and methods to close them.

## BUFFER OVERFLOWS

Applications reside in memory during operation. Poorly written software can inadvertently include code that attempts to store data beyond the boundaries assigned to the buffer. The result is that the program will overwrite data in adjacent memory locations, causing incorrect results or a crash. Such undesirable behavior can be triggered by an attacker who writes code that will perform such a buffer overflow. Depending on the design of the system and its ability to prevent such a data excursion or recover from the error, an attacker may open various exploitation capabilities that are a consequence of the crash.

In addition to writing data in adjacent memory locations, a sophisticated attacker can also create a malicious program that will overwrite the return address present on the stack. Upon completion of execution, a program retrieves the return address and proceeds to that location to continue running code. By overwriting the return address with an address that exists within the attack code, the program will obediently branch to the incorrect address and continue processing the attack code. A similar technique can be used by overwriting a function pointer. In both cases, the program has been diverted to perform the attacker's code.

Buffer-overflow attacks can be minimized by writing code that carefully checks the bounds of allocated memory against the requested memory-write process to prevent excursions beyond the allocated space. This function can also be provided by a well-designed compiler.

## MEMORY POINTER ATTACKS

In a standard computer environment in which the memory-access privileges of applications are not enforced or restricted to application-specific bounds, memory pointers can be used by an attacker to redirect execution to malicious code. In this environment, memory pointers can point to any memory address. By placing malicious code at addresses commonly used by the operating system, an attacker can divert the OS to perform malicious functions without detection.

An application dynamically allocates and releases memory at run-time. This memory is referred to as the "heap," and it usually includes data being used by the program. Data in the heap can be used by attackers in a somewhat different manner than a buffer-overflow attack. In particular, heap data include data structures that often include pointers.

## THE IMPACT OF MEMORY-MANAGEMENT ATTACKS

Not only do memory exploits compromise the security of the target application, but they can also compromise the security of the target computer. Moreover, such an attack can also compromise the security of an entire network if its security policies, firewalls, and sharing of drives have not been administered properly. It is critical that an organization take steps to protect it against such attacks, since the impact may have far-reaching consequences.

## MINIMIZING MEMORY-MANAGEMENT ATTACKS

There is no substitute for secure programming practices. It is also inadvisable to rely solely on the compiler or run-time operating system to catch memory errors. Programmers need to ensure that memory management is being handled properly. The allocation, use, erasure, and subsequent release of dynamic memory must not be left to chance.

Secure memory management begins with good security-minded programming practices. Although not a comprehensive list, the following comprises a reasonable representation of practices that will ultimately produce better memory management within applications:

- Minimize the use of memory pointers.
- Destroy memory pointers immediately after use.
- Always allocate and release (free) memory within the same software module to minimize the possibility that memory will be forgotten.
- Release memory only once.
- Do not rely upon the operating system to clean memory—erase the contents of allocated memory before releasing.
- If global variables are used to store memory pointers, reset their contents to null after release of the related memory.
- Make sure that the amount of memory requested by the allocation command is within the bounds allowed.

- Check to assure that the amount of memory being requested in an allocation will be large enough for the projected use.
- Write code so that allocation errors are handled.
- Initialize allocated memory within the code, rather than relying upon the operating system to do so.

## PLATFORM-DESIGN CONSIDERATIONS

Attackers will seek to employ whatever techniques are available to obtain access to secure information (cryptographic keys, etc.). Although it is desirable that application developers employ best practices for secure memory management in order to prevent the use of their application for such attacks, platform developers cannot assume that this will always be the case. Therefore, techniques to create walls in memory between different operating applications will be a good first step in minimizing memory excursions beyond the bounds allocated to a specific application. The use of trusted platform module (TPM) technology (Chapter 8) will also help identify compromised systems and prevent the inadvertent trusting of such compromised platforms.

## TRUSTED EXECUTION TECHNOLOGY

The characteristics of a hardware-based security system include attestation, process isolation, tamper-resistant storage of core secrets, and secure IO paths. Using a mixture of these hardware-based protection techniques, Intel recently launched a secure computing initiative. Initially code-named LaGrande, the technology has been renamed the trusted execution technology (TET or TXT). TET is Intel's attempt to create a trusted platform. It provides a specification that defines how the TET hardware can be used to extend the trusted platform to include operating systems created by developers who employ the technology.

Paying attention to attack vectors on memory and IO devices, Intel has added hardware improvements and partitioning of secure space from all other space. Developers must be careful to follow Intel's specs in order to maximize the protection and added trust offered by the technology.

The categories of enhanced protection offered by TET are listed below with a brief description of the conceptual goal for each.

## Protected Execution

In order to prevent unauthorized applications from gaining access to any information associated with a protected application, this capability isolates each application, its memory space, its return vectors, etc. This should limit or prevent the ability of unauthorized applications from altering information in the protected application.

## Protected Storage

Using the TPM (described in Chapter 8), the TET system encrypts and stores keys and any sensitive data within the physically protected boundaries of the device. Not only are the TPM's mechanisms employed to protect this information, but the encryption keys used to protect the data also include information about the trustworthiness of the environment as an element of their creation. Should an untrustworthy environment be detected at a later date, this implementation will prevent the release of keys or other protected data from within the TPM.

## Protected Input

Communication between the processor and external devices, such as a keyboard, mouse, or USB device, can be compromised by malicious code. TET seeks to close this attack channel by introducing encryption between the processor and the external device, using keys that have been created in a trusted environment and that are stored in the TPM. This will prevent unauthorized persons from observing user typing activity (usually achieved through the use of keystroke-capture software), mouse movements, or communications with a USB device. On the processor side, each application must be enabled to accommodate the decryption process, thereby creating a secure channel between the external device and the application (with keys stored within the TPM).

## Protected Graphics

Screen captures and fake screens are eliminated by the TET system through the use of the protected execution environment. By creating rigid boundaries between applications and then allowing only trusted applications operating within the protected environment to gain access to the display-frame buffer, the ability of attackers to obtain (through the use of a screen-capture program) data from the display buffer is eliminated. Moreover, data displayed on the screen is only possible from the trusted application running within the protected environment. This eliminates pathways by which false screens can be displayed. Much like the protected input, this approach creates an encrypted and protected path between the application and the display.

### Environment Authentication and Protected Launch

Following the specifications of the TCG for correctly invoking a trusted environment, the TET system measures the software and hardware environment during the bootstrap process to assure than no components have been compromised. The hash-code signatures of trusted hardware and software components have been stored in the TPM after being measured in a trusted environment before shipping and are compared to the signatures seen by the system during bootstrap. Using the processes described in previous chapters of this book, the TET system uses signature comparisons to control the launch of trusted applications and establishes the level of trust before communication with other platforms.

### Domain Manager

The TET system introduces a domain manager whose function is to manage the interaction of the hardware that is running in a specific instantiation of a protected environment with the software applications (also within the same environment) that require the interaction. A separate TET domain manager is invoked for each protected environment. In order to enforce separation of environments, domain managers cannot access one another's data, hardware, or other information.

### Platform and Hardware Requirements

In order to perform the security functions described above, the TET system must employ various hardware modules to achieve the desired security. At the very least, a TET-enabled system requires a properly implemented (and initialized) TPM, processor, keyboard, mouse, and display.

The need for a specialized processor stems from the requirement that the system be able to create multiple, isolated execution environments. This will provide the user with the option of running any specific application in a standard partition or in a protected partition. As explained above, the latter option isolates the application from all others and protects its resources from access by any other application. Access by the application to certain resources (the display, keyboard, and mouse, for example) is protected by bidirectional encryption. Moreover, the specialized processor enforces domain separation, memory protection, and event handling. It must offer secure (encrypted) pathways to memory, graphics, keyboard, mouse, and the TPM.

Complementary hardware changes must, of course, be present on the related peripheral devices such as the keyboard, mouse, and display. With encrypted pathways between the processor and these devices, attacks that capture keystrokes, mouse clicks, or screen information should be defeated. Since the TPM is platform-specific from the moment of initialization by a trusted party (say, at the factory), changes to sensitive configuration elements (both hardware and software) will be detected. Moreover, the TPM provides physical and electronic protection of cryptographic keys, specific signatures and certificates, user-specific sensitive data, and (ideally) hardware-based key and random-number generation within a tamper-protected enclosure. As explained in the previous chapter, data that is protected by the TPM cannot be accessed unless the system is in a specified state and authorized commands have been issued.

Users need not employ the security features of the TET system in running their applications. Intel has designed the system so that users can elect to execute applications in a completely open and untrusted environment, as they do today. That is, the standard partition is identical to the manner in which applications are executed in today's unprotected environment. This standard partition provides a migration path, allowing existing applications that do not have the TET-required features to be executed as they are before users obtain the security-enhanced releases of the applications. By the same token, the TPM must be configured to require user election in order to activate the TPM system.

In addition to allowing users to employ their existing non-TPM-enabled applications on these new platforms as they have in the past, TET also enforces the control of the user over the invocation of the trusted environments and therefore the possible sharing of information with remote computers or authorities when trust needs to be established. This is consistent with the points on user privacy and control raised in Chapter 8.

Should a user elect to run an application in a protected environment, a parallel, coexisting environment (partition) will be created that runs TET-supported software and employs the new hardware. As explained above, applications running in this environment are completely isolated from one another and cannot view or access one another's memory, display, keyboard, or mouse data. The hardware components required to achieve this include the TET-enabled processor and related IO chips required to encrypt and decrypt data from the keyboard, mouse, display, and any other TET-protected attachments. The TET domain manager enforces the isolation and protection of separate partitions.

Applications need not be limited to either protected or unprotected mode. For example, applications can be developed that employ both environments, where IO functions might be handled in the unprotected partition while the core, security-sensitive applications would be handled within a protected partition.

Of course, before the TET-protected environment can be loaded, the initial trust of the hardware and software modules must be established during the bootstrap process. The TET system provides three different paths for this.

First, a user may decide to trust the initial configuration that has been delivered to him by the manufacturer or supplier. The user can create a secret phrase that only he knows and then seal this phrase into the initial trusted environment (within the TPM). The TET system provides the user with the ability to request and view the stored phrase upon booting. Any change to the trusted environment (through its examination of module hash codes within the PCM) would be intercepted and the secret message (or any other TPM-protected secrets) would not be available. The user would know immediately that the system cannot be trusted due to some change in these security-critical modules.

A second option employs a pluggable device (such as a USB or PCM-CIA device) that contains the measurements of the modules that were present during the trusted initial configuration. This device can then be used to measure the system independent of the TPM's result and provide the user with the results of the trust measurement.

A third option is the extension of the second option to a remote party (that is, the use of a remote party to provide the validation of trustworthiness of the system's modules). Although this offers the advantage of remoteness (and the consequent difficulty of an attacker successfully compromising both the system and the remotely stored attributes), it introduces concerns about the protection of the communication channel between the two parties or the possible absence of the remote party due to network or local power problems. Reporting of the results would ideally be delivered through some independent path (a back channel) such as a web page or telephone dialup.

The TET system as implemented does not require reboot of the platform in order to establish a protected partition. In order to achieve this, the invocation of the protection turns off all running processes and begins the authentication of hardware and software modules as if the system were proceeding with a reboot. The process is comparable to an authenticated bootstrap process but differs in that any running processes are suspended, thereby allowing the authentication of elements to proceed without any possible interference from other processes. Upon successful completion, a protected partition is created and prior processes are allowed to proceed in the unprotected space. During release of a protected partition, the domain manager handles cleanup and release of memory and pointers and then finally terminates itself.

### Unplanned Events

It is possible that either a loss of power or an unexpected system reset may occur while a protected partition exists. Although the CPU might become unavailable, the contents of memory may remain intact. TET employs one of two actions to protect secret information in either of these situations. First, memory access is blocked upon reset or power loss, and, second, memory gets zeroed upon restoration of power. In the event that an unexpected "sleep" command has been received by the platform, the TET system encrypts all data in memory before releasing control to the hibernate or power-down sequence. On power-up, the encrypted pages can be decrypted and execution resumed if all other pointers are still valid. Otherwise, the user may need to restart his protected session.

### Privacy and User Control

As explained above, the TET system gives the user complete control over whether or not the protected partitions will be employed for any application and the extent to which the application might reside in both protected and unprotected partitions. This is consistent with the user-privacy concept presented at the end of Chapter 8. The activation or deactivation of TET features and functions can only be performed with the complete knowledge of the user, thereby granting him control over his privacy. Moreover, the user maintains knowledge and control over any system-trust evaluations that are transmitted over any network.

In keeping with this philosophy of user control and knowledge, systems that include TET are shipped with the TET system disabled (deactivated). In order to enable it, the user must give specific permission and take direct action. The user is able to employ certain security features within the TPM (such as cryptographic modules) without being required to enable remote authentication of the system's trust (attestation). Moreover, keys, attestation, and the TPM must not be used in a manner that compromises the user's privacy without his knowledge and prior approval.

# Chapter 8

## THE TRUSTED PLATFORM MODULE

### THE NEED FOR INCREASED NETWORK AND PC SECURITY

When they were first developed, general-purpose personal computers were not designed with security and trust as an integral part of the architecture. After all, computers then were completely stand-alone—data was transferred only through sharing of disks, which at that time was a relatively safe and trustworthy process. The Internet was developed by people who saw great potential in being able to share scientific and military information quickly and easily between computers. Security and the need for trust did not surface until viruses began to spread by disk, and, more significantly, these open computers were attached to networks. When networking was created back in the 1980s, it primarily served a function of enhanced communication and sharing of information between researchers within a laboratory or university department. As networking grew, it began to form connections between buildings, then between different universities, and ultimately between widely disparate organizations spanning the globe. As networking expanded, so did the realization that this new medium of interconnectivity introduced a significant degree of anonymity to the remote parties. Users were relying on trust. As viruses began to spread using these networks, the reliance on trust began to fade, and users sought ways to protect their computers and data. Moreover, as they are currently designed and implemented, if a user has access to a person's private information (for example, his online medical records at a hospital), he is completely free to copy that person's information and retransmit it to anyone anywhere. There is no inherited access control in today's Internet or PC file system.

Even with basic password protection implemented on a system, a simple screen-capture or keystroke-capture program, installed without the user's knowledge, can seize sensitive information in the background and forward it to a malicious attacker.

A class of attack software that resides at the root of a PC is called a rootkit. The rootkit software resides in a hidden location on a PC without the user being aware of its presence. Rootkits hide themselves by modifying the operating system itself. This allows them to survive reboots of the system. They can replace normal system utility routines, adding their specific attack function to processes that are used frequently by the average user. This class of attack software can perform any of a number of malicious acts, including capturing and forwarding passwords, sending spam email designed to identify new attack targets, direct attacking of other machines on the local network, or opening a remote-control function that can be used by the attacker. Since local area networks are designed to allow easy communication between PCs and enable file and printer sharing, entire organizations are often placed at risk once a rootkit has been established on any one of the machines in the office. Depending on the nature of the business, this may introduce legal liability due to the potential loss of private user information.

Rootkits are now quite common and readily available on several web sites. They have become sufficiently easy to use that nonexpert users can develop them using such available software packages. The nastier versions employ virtualization techniques (such as those used by legitimate companies like VMWare) in which a normal OS runs. This gives the rootkit access to all information while evading detection.

Botnets (from "robot network") are becoming an increasingly common attack mode. In this type of attack, a virus is placed on the target computer that allows a hacker to remotely command the computer to perform any of a number of functions. The network robots can launch denial-of-service attacks on targeted computers, send spam emails to members of the mailing lists present on each machine, or capture and forward password and account information to the attacker. Botnets consisting of thousands of computers are not uncommon, making them a very effective means to launch denial-of-service attacks. Computers infected with botnet software are particularly dangerous to systems that employ trust, since they tend to undermine the trust of all of the computers that include the commandeered computer as a member of the trusted circle. It is estimated that one in every four computers worldwide has a botnet infection.

## TRUST

Current computer systems and networks employ an unspoken hierarchy of trust. When logging into a business's website to enter personal information, the user must decide if he trusts that remote business to protect his information. The user must also decide if he trusts the business to have properly protected itself against viruses and Trojan horses. Even if the answer is "yes" to both, he must also decide if he trusts the business's employees to protect his information. By the same token, can the business's affiliates be trusted to protect his information? All of these "trust" decisions must be made by the user, often without much supporting information.

Organizations that claim to protect private user information must have a mechanism in place to enforce that protection. Moreover, the organization must have a mechanism in place to enforce the policy amongst its affiliates who might have access to that information.

Ultimately, a system must be "trusted" to behave the way the user expects it to behave, including the manner in which information is being protected. Once such a system has been established and the user community at large accepts the system as being truly "trustworthy," its extension to the networked world is straightforward. Trusted machines that can demonstrate their trustworthiness to the satisfaction of the broad user community can then limit trusted functions to other platforms that have similarly established themselves as trusted. Platforms that are not trusted can be separated and treated as suspect.

The means to establish trust is the central issue of this chapter.

## THE NEED FOR A TRUSTED PLATFORM MODULE

Today, the movement towards increased mobility by the technology workforce increases the demand for secure and trusted communication over networks. Remote workers have the ability to maintain productivity while far from their home office, accessing data and support information remotely. As a result, the hosting systems back at the home office must employ technologies that protect against unauthorized users trying to gain access. Web interfaces must be carefully secured against bugs and vulnerabilities.

Electronic commerce, such as online bill paying, fund transfers, and other banking functions, has increased dramatically in the past decade. Shopping online and subsequent purchasing of goods now rivals "brick and mortar" stores during holiday seasons.

This increased dependence on electronic networks further heightens the urgency for hardware-based protection of information, authentication of users, and establishment of high degrees of trust in local and remote computing systems. The economic impact of failure to protect such information is demonstrated almost daily by the loss of private information, identity theft, and hacking.

This unprotected, nontrusted environment needs a low-cost module that is tamper-evident and can protect central security information (such as cryptographic keys) against theft or alteration by attackers. With this capability, a system could, in principle, measure the integrity of the hardware and software modules resident on the system and create certificates that certify those modules using techniques described in Chapters 4, 5, and 6.

Such a module cannot be software-based, since such solutions cannot possibly provide protection against physical attacks. A security module that establishes trust that can be inherited by its software and hardware modules must be hardware-based. Moreover, such a module should be low-cost, and a process must be established to assure that it can only be deployed on systems that are worthy of trust. Failure to do so would cause a contaminated system to assert itself as "trustworthy," and its impact on other systems could possibly spread. The hardware module should be dedicated and independent of the host operating system during its security operations.

## THE CONCEPT OF TRUSTED COMPUTING

The term "trusted computing" is a general term used by the IT industry when referring to the creation of platforms (PCs, etc.) that have special hardware whose function includes cryptography, validation, and authentication of hardware and software modules and certification of the trustworthiness of the platform to the user and other remote devices. This hardware element also aids in the protection of secure data within the device.

Through its ability to control the execution of processes (preventing untrusted processes or at least notifying the user that they are not trusted), trusted computing systems should prevent viruses and piracy. But there is an additional concern, raised by privacy-rights groups and others, that the entire trusted-computing paradigm will reside in the hands of a few large manufacturers. Currently, the technical and policy standards regarding trusted computing are handled by a consortium of large manufacturers of electronics and software (such as Microsoft, IBM, HP, Intel, AMD, and others). User groups have formed to ask for regulation of trusted computing (and others have asked for its outright rejection), but there is little movement in these deliberations at this time.

## THE TRUSTED PLATFORM MODULE

In 1999, a group of leading IT and PC companies created the Trusted Computing Platform Alliance (TCPA[1]). The founding members included Compaq, Hewlett-Packard, IBM, Intel, and Microsoft. This group set as its objective a definition of a trusted computing platform with special attention to ensuring privacy and security.

It should be noted that there are groups[2] that are opposed to the TCPA approach, citing privacy rights, freedom of speech, and other concerns.

Any system that employs trust must ultimately rely upon a person or group of people that must be trusted. When examined carefully, all systems have at their root an administrator, programmer, or manufacturer that must be declared trustworthy. To the extent that this is not true, all of the subsequent trust dependencies fall. It is probably best to establish that trust by using groups of people rather than a single person. It is less likely that all of the people in a group will agree to deliver compromised systems (this would be a conspiracy), but of course nothing can ever be guaranteed. At some point, trust-based systems rely on people.

At its core, the group defined a trusted platform module (TPM), which would handle all software- and hardware-related security features, including storage and protection of keys, auditing of surrounding hardware and software components, and creation of certificates of trust that can then be viewed either remotely by administrators or employed as part of any associated trusted process. The TPM must, by its nature, employ very high security tools to protect its keys, certificates, and other security-related contents. It must protect this information against unauthorized external access, physical and software attacks, and replacement by altered or otherwise copied versions of the TPM. In doing so, it establishes a root of trust at a fundamental level of the computing system.

The TPM assumes that software must be isolated from outside interference in order to be trusted. Moreover, it assumes that proper behavior implies trust. This carries the implicit assumption that all possible behaviors have been tested—failure to do so could allow the existence of a path for compromise.

The TCPA defined a core root of trust (CRT) as its most basic building block from which all trust is derived for a specific PC. In order to protect that fundamental role, the CRT is required to be a static portion of code that is a component of the platform's initialization routine. It must be executed first as part of the bootstrap process. (See Chapter 6 and Figure 6.1.) This places the machine in a known initial state that can be compared to a trusted initial state that has been independently confirmed.

Since software alone cannot be protected against physical attacks, the TPM must be a hardware device, such as an application-specific integrated circuit (ASIC) or dedicated chip on the motherboard of the platform. With these two constraints (CRT and physical device), the TPM becomes the root from which all trust is built for the platform.

A proper implementation of the TPM must include strong physical protection (tamper evidence and tamper resistance) so that its contents are protected against physical attack. As mentioned above, the cryptographic keys that control critical resources (root access, secure memory routines, administration functions, etc.) must be stored within the TPM. Ideally, a true random-number generator would reside within the TPM (to be distinguished from software-based pseudo-random-number generators), and associated functions such as critical cryptography, hashing, and the creation of digital signatures or certificates should be performed within the TPM bounds. Data traveling into and out of the TPM should be cryptographically secure. The TPM should be not only physically bound to the host platform but also bound through manufacturer-owned signed digital certificates that are stored at the time of initialization at the factory so that swapping of the TPM module would be easily detected. Keys never leave the TPM, and data of any sort that is protected by the TPM can only be decrypted when the system is in a specified state and a specific authorized command is issued.

The startup of the TPM has three basic options:

- Clear: the TPM is requested to start with default values that have been set by the TPM owner.

- State: The TPM is instructed to recover some previously saved state and continue operations from this state.

- Deactivate: The TPM is turned off and will not process any further commands until the reset command is issued by the TPM owner.

## Structure of the TPM

The architecture of the TPM, as specified by the TCG, requires that a trusted platform execute a specific series of steps upon power-up. First, the CRT must be authenticated. Since the CRT resides at the most fundamental level of a trusted platform, this step is critical. If the CRT is authentic, then the secure bootstrap process executes the instructions contained within the CRT. This process feeds forward—the executed steps determine the validity of subsequent steps and proceed to execute those in turn. This maintains the "known state" condition of the system during the boot process.

In the event that the authentication steps fail at any point, there are two options. First, the system can be shut down. This is generally not the option of choice, since it leaves the user completely without functionality. The second option is to allow the system to complete its startup process but leave it in a state that cannot be trusted (unauthenticated). In this second option, none of the secure information can be accessed, but the user retains some basic level of functionality.

This TPM structure enables the CRT to establish authentication of itself, its modules and hardware, and, to some extent, software applications. The creation of this authenticated state allows the platform to join a worldwide network of trusted platforms, thereby creating a network of more secure machines. To the extent that secure memory management and input/output control is included (Chapters 4 and 7), the trust is strengthened by forcing the isolation of applications and their allocated memory, thereby avoiding exposure to buffer-overflow attacks and other attack vectors that employ memory techniques.

Each TPM includes a 2048-bit RSA key pair (the endorsement key, or EK) that is created before delivery to the end user. When the EK is created, a credential is also created that can be used to verify the validity of the EK. The TPM is designed to prevent alternation or subsequent generation of EKs once configuration has been completed at the factory. The private key portion of the EK can never leave the TPM or be viewed outside of the protected confines of the hardware module.

The EK is used for verification of the initial state of the TPM and is bound to the platform. It acts as a root of trust for reporting when remote attestation is invoked. The system also creates attestation identity keys (AIKs) that are based upon the EK and can be created by the owner at any time. The user can create multiple AIK identities, thereby allowing enhanced privacy, using different identities for different operations. Since the EK is platform-specific, the AIK cannot be migrated from one platform to another.

The TPM must be shipped without an owner. Initialization of the TPM by the end user should require his physical presence, and he must reset all old secrets (excluding the platform-specific EK).

Since the TPM hardware includes secure storage combined with tamper resistance, the storage of keys and other user-critical information enjoys the protection afforded by a hardware solution.

**The TPM's Primary Roles**

Since the primary role of the TPM is to act as the root of trust for the platform, it must check and verify the integrity of the system's hardware and software during the boot process. Armed with this, it should provide authentication and status information to local and remote (authenticated) administrators as well as to software programs that request such information. It must provide a secure storage location for the user's private keys and private data and control over these items to the authenticated user. Some cautionary notes are in order here.

The functionality of the TPM does not span all of the security/integrity-related functions. For example, the TPM relies upon the host system for information regarding host software. In checking the integrity of the host software, the TPM posts a request to the host, which then proceeds to "measure" the integrity of the identified software. The TPM does not have a means to independently verify that the host measured the requested software.

The TPM does not have control over the PC's hardware functionality. That is, the TPM cannot demand a physical reset of the PC, nor is it able to prevent programs from accessing portions of the PC's memory. The latter must be provided by a proper implementation of secure memory management. (See Chapter 7.)

The user controls the activation/deactivation of the TPM. When deactivated, the user's PC is not trusted, nor are any of its applications or its communications with the outside world (such as over the Internet).

Ownership of the TPM is not the same as a "super user"—the TPM can be deactivated, and ownership does not automatically grant access to all operations. All protected operations require authorization. The owner and users control the use of all keys stored within the TPM.

The owner must not foster a false sense of security about the protection of encrypted data on his hard drive. Data encrypted on the user's hard drive using encryption keys that are stored within the TPM are no stronger than the strength of the keys themselves. Although the keys are stored in physically secure memory within the TPM, which provides a heightened degree of protection, dictionary attacks and other hacking techniques side-step the acquisition of the cryptographic keys and instead rely upon brute-force methods to guess the key. Therefore, it is incumbent upon the user to employ strong cryptographic keys, generated using the techniques described earlier in this book, with the maximum key lengths allowed by the system.

Technological solutions, whether hardware- or software-based, do not prevent a malicious user from simply writing down information from the screen and passing it on to others.

## TPM and Rootkits

Although there are a variety of rootkit detection and removal tools available, these require continual vigilance by the user, running the detector frequently, adding it to scheduled tasks, etc. The TCG has devoted resources to the development of standards that provide significant protection against rootkits.

As explained above, when the PC boots, the TPM measures the BIOS, the boot loader, any critical applications within the operating system, critical hardware devices, etc. Since these measurements were made at the time of manufacture at a trusted location (the point of origin of the PC) and stored within secure, immutable memory within the TPM, any changes to the signatures are immediately detected. The system is flagged as not trustworthy, and the user is so notified. The recommendation is that the PC be repaired.

## Complications Introduced by TPM

As explained above, the most effective TPM is one which has been bound to the specific hardware and software configuration that was present at the time it was initialized. The owner subsequently assumed responsibility for the TPM. Keys, software hash codes, and user permissions were bound to the original platform configuration.

Hardware devices fail, and depending on which device has failed, there may be complications introduced by the presence of the TPM system. Similar issues arise with hardware upgrades. In the event of hard-drive failure or corruption of files, the user may have no choice but to remove and replace the hard drive or otherwise replace critical files with restored files. This most likely will require the owner to perform individual backup and restore operations though the TPM, effecting a manual migration to the new configuration. This can be time-consuming and may present an opportunity for errors or oversights.

The motherboard itself might fail. There must be a migration path of data from one TPM to another, although it should be a requirement that the source and target motherboards be the same model and manufacturer. This will likely require an approval step by the manufacturer.

Cryptographic keys that were used to encrypt files on the (failed) hard drive will have to be migrated to the new drive, along with the images of the encrypted files. This will require authorization of migration by the owner and subsequent acceptance of migration by the user (who may or may not be the same person).

Migration to a new PC for upgrade purposes similarly will require that the owner authorize the migration. In the case of a single platform with multiple users, each user will subsequently have to consent to the migration individually. This introduces an administrative burden that can be minimized by a carefully architected TPM application interface, but even such an interface will not eliminate the approval stage.

### Residual Vulnerabilities

The introduction of TPM technology onto the motherboard of a platform raises the degree of protection and trust that can be ascribed to the system. Nonetheless, there remain some obvious paths of attack that are not addressed by TPM.

Access to the frame buffer that drives the user's display is an attack avenue that is not addressed by the TPM. In this attack, the attacker accesses the video memory buffer and captures screen shots of the user's work. Hardware protection against this form of attack has been described in previous chapters of this book (see Chapter 4).

Memory can often be accessed in unprotected systems through the use of DMA commands or buffer overflows. Proper secure memory management (see Chapter 7) will protect against this type of attack.

Key-capture routines are not detected or eliminated by TPM. Steps that can be taken to protect against this form of attack have been described in Chapter 4.

TPM currently employs SHA-1 in creating nonreversible hash-code summaries of software modules and other information it wishes to authenticate at a later date. Unfortunately, as explained in earlier chapters, SHA-1 was recently broken by hackers. This raises immediate concerns about the strength of TPM against attacks. The use of SHA-1 by TPM should be replaced as soon as possible by a stronger hash algorithm (such as secure hash algorithm 256, or SHA 256), which has been certified by the National Security Agency.

## Privacy and Digital Rights Management

To the extent that a TPM implementation includes the protection of user's digital-rights-management ("DRM") keys, it is appropriate to review the issues surrounding this controversial topic.

The protection of a user's privacy, creating a trusted platform, and limiting a user's access to information have created some emotionally charged debates in recent years. Security and privacy are often interpreted as attempts to address the same thing.

For clarity, throughout this book, the term "security" means the protection of information assets through the use of technology. "Privacy" means a user's right to be able to choose when personal data is collected, used, or shared. Clearly one must employ security to achieve privacy, but the desire of a user to protect his privacy using security does not give other parties the right to collect, use, or share that user's private information without his consent.

One problem that has enjoyed a great deal of scrutiny is the theft and distribution of copyrighted material that is owned by a content creator (a music label or motion-picture company, for example). In addition to the music and motion-picture industries, the theft of software is not far behind on the list of providers concerned about such theft. In response to this problem, these industries have created digital-rights-management (DRM) technology, which seeks to control the ability of users to make or otherwise distribute copies of music, movies, and software. Although effective, DRM is viewed by some users as awkward and limiting and by others as an invasion of their privacy. In the music field, for example, users have been long accustomed to being able to purchase (for example) a record album and then make copies of specific songs (or the entire album) onto other media, such as audio tapes or MP3 players. Some users feel that once they have purchased the album, they are free to copy it as they choose. In effect, these users feel that, once purchased, the album becomes personal data.

The digital world introduces a new twist to this concept, however. In the case of a record album, the users are purchasing a reasonable copy of the original music (which was mixed and recorded onto master tapes from which the albums are subsequently "cut"). The rendering of the music onto an album suffers some alteration of the spectral content of the audio tracks. Records are not an exact duplicate of the original recording.

If the studios create digitized copies that are then burned onto compact disks, these copies are as close to a true replication of the original music as possible (limited perhaps by the conversion of analog tape tracks to digital format). If the original recordings are captured digitally and recorded in digital form, the subsequent copies are likely to be an even closer approximation of the original content.

Digital copies subsequently burned onto CDs do not lose any of the integrity offered by the original CD, unless compression technology was employed to reduce the storage space required per track (as is the case with MP3 files, which employ compression at the expense of fidelity). The propagation of these copies is largely viewed by the music industry as lost revenue; it asserts that all of the illegal copies would have been purchased had proper DRM technology been implemented. Others argue that these illegal copies were obtained due to their low or nonexistent cost. Had these same people been required to purchase legitimate copies, it is argued, these users would likely not have purchased the content at all. The true lost revenue lies somewhere between these two extremes.

DRM introduces encryption keys and certificates that can be bound to specific platforms or players, and copies can be limited to that platform only. DRM usually includes a migration path so that users can enjoy their music on other platforms, but the migration disables the music on the previous platform. In the most common implementation, only one platform can play DRM-protected content at any given time. DRM-protected music was initially widely used by the music industry, but complaints by users regarding the awkward restrictions caused a gradual withdrawal from its use. Online purchases of MP3 music files were estimated at somewhere between 10 and 20 percent of all music sales revenue in 2007, so the music industry tends to be responsive to customer demands regarding the use of DRM in the purchased files. The motion-picture industry has also introduced DRM technology to limit copying of digital movies to backup versions only. Microsoft has introduced a form of DRM into document control, allowing the creator to control the ability of others to print or forward the file to others.

Another issue that is often voiced with respect to DRM is the user's privacy. Some groups argue that the purchase of music or movie content should remain anonymous, protecting the user's privacy. User groups often voice concerns about the invasion of privacy regarding DRM implementations that employ information about the user. There are fears that the migration process is equivalent to a tracking system that records what platforms are being used by which users for specific content.

Finally, there is a concern amongst some users that the owners of software applications could conceivably track a user's migration of purchased software as it is moved from one platform to another. Some users assert that information and content (such as software) should not be protected from their legitimate owners. Rather, it is felt that the legitimate owners should have full control over their purchased content.

The issues surrounding control and privacy often get mixed with the trust and privacy issues that are being addressed by TPM. As a result, some users are reluctant to employ the technology for fear that the originating organization might track or otherwise seek to control access of users of their products. This fear has fostered a mistrust of any technology that touches user privacy.

### Concluding Observations on TPM

The use of hardware-based system authentication and verification on booting of a platform by the TPM technology is a solid step forward towards the development of systems that are secure against hacking and theft of sensitive information. By moving the functionality of TPM to the root level during the boot process and employing careful practices to initialize such systems with trusted software, firmware, and hardware, TPM will likely provide a solid foundation upon which other hardware-based security technologies can be built.

Issues and concerns remain that need to be addressed. At this time, there is nothing to assure a user that the TPM system will allow him to run applications produced by a competitor of the system's manufacturer. Content providers could, in principle, examine the elements reported within the attestation and refuse service or content to users who are running competitive applications or parallel operating systems.

Manufacturers or software providers could conceivably use the remote attestation to require the user to pay some charge in order to enable the operation of such competing software. Such fees could be asked of the application developers themselves in order to allow their applications to run on the systems.

TPM's strong, hardware-based protection of secrets could act as a double-edged sword, preventing users and bonafide government agencies alike from verifying what is actually occurring within the TPM validation process. How would a user truly know that the TPM is actually checking and not simply returning a conclusion that the system should be trusted? How can users convince themselves that there are no back doors in the code or the TPM itself?

How will users be able to exercise their rights to fair use of legally purchased DRM-protected content? Will migration paths be provided for the originals and the legal copies?

On the sensitive matter of user privacy, a user's privacy is best protected by introducing and employing carefully conceived and tested hardware-based security technologies. Programmers must be careful to consider user privacy during the development of these applications. Such applications should protect user content and allow ease of use by rightful owners, preferably without resorting to tracking of user activities. The determination of a user's identity through hardware security technologies (as opposed to software-only applications) should be sufficiently unique that the user will be confident that spoofing cannot occur. Legal recourse can be added to complement but not replace properly implemented hardware security technologies. The use of independent, nonprofit monitoring and enforcement organizations should be considered as a means to defuse the user community's concerns that the technology only serves to protect the creators of software. Finally, the user should be notified of the intent to share or transmit his personal information, and his approval must be granted before such sharing can occur.

## REFERENCES

[1] See http://www.trustedcomputing.org.
[2] See htpp://www.againsttcpa.com.

# Chapter 9

## FIELD-PROGRAMMABLE GATE ARRAYS

**BACKGROUND**

Before programmable logic was developed, circuits requiring a fixed logical process were constructed on dedicated boards using basic building-block chips and associated interface devices. Sufficiently mature boards that required cost or size reduction due to high expected volumes were subsequently embedded in application-specific integrated circuits (ASICs). Unfortunately, ASICs are relatively easy to attack. They are not based on identical building blocks with switches that are turned on to create pathways but rather are made of easily recognized components. It is possible to strip off the top of an ASIC chip and copy its layout easily.

In contrast, a field-programmable gate array (FPGA) is a form of integrated circuit that consists of a large number of identical building blocks, each of which can be configured to perform specific functions. These building blocks communicate with one another through interconnection matrices and programmable switches that can be configured to create or close communication paths between these building blocks. As designs for higher-level functions are perfected, these can be used in subsequent designs wherein the previous functions are complemented with additional functions to perform progressively more complex operations. Like software (or a child's building blocks), they can be reconfigured into new applications, creating a growing library of functions.

At its most primitive level, an FPGA consists of logic cells. Each logic cell contains a path for some small number of inputs that are then subjected to Boolean logic per the programmer's desire. Some cells include a lookup table (LUT) in which input is converted directly to some output, as in Figure 9.1.

In operation, the input value (in the example above, the input value is 3) is used as an index to the lookup table. The contents of address 3 within the table (in this example, 27) are then substituted and become the output value. By changing the contents of the LUT, a programmer can change input values to output values that he defines. LUTs are often used for false color transformations, gamma corrections (in which the effects of a display or printer are corrected), and logic transformations (as in the FPGA). The cost of using such a flexible LUT is a delay, incurred as the lookup process occurs.

The term "field-programmable" refers to the fact that a manufacturer delivers a block of undefined modules which are then "programmed" by the user, who turns on and off wiring switches to define the flow of data and sets the values of lookup tables or other logic components in order to achieve his desired function. The result is then "burned into" the FPGA, either in the programmer's facility or in the field using special burning software. The technology supports both semi-permanent and permanent (one-time) burning operations. In situations where the FPGA is to be employed for security applications, it is most likely that the core security functions will be burned permanently, whereas memory space in which keys are stored will be semi-permanent, allowing only authorized applications to change the content.

## WHY USE AN FPGA?

In addition to its obvious flexibility for customization, the FPGA technology is hardware. As such, it offers the possibility of providing physical protection of security functions. By adding tamper-evident and tamper-

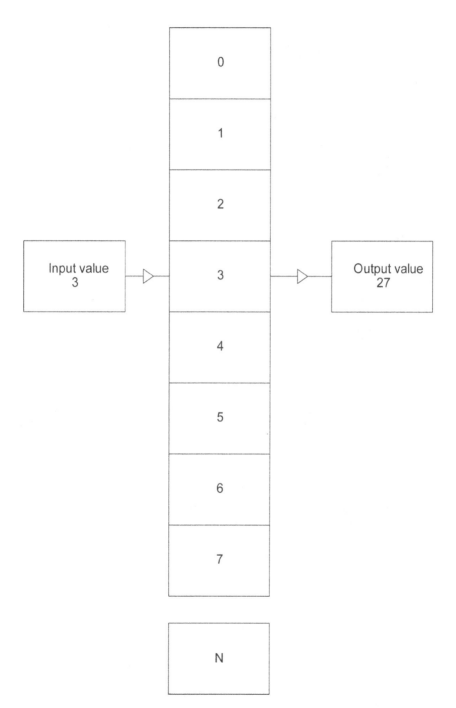

**Figure 9.1**  Operation of a Lookup Table (LUT).

resistant packaging technologies, the FPGA may provide the correct platform for such security functions.

FPGAs have the ability to execute secure programs, protect data and code from unauthorized access, and secure IO channels. Moreover, since the FPGA programs are burned into the device, recovery to a predefined state is automatic. Hardware-based processing through the modules results in high performance operation (low latency/delays).

There are many reasons that FPGA technology is being considered and/or deployed:

- Protection of data (software, research results, designs, creative efforts)
- Protection of personal and transaction information during e-commerce
- Protection of system secrets (keys, passwords, etc.)
- Protection against attacks (ATMs, gambling machines, etc.)
- TPM authentication and attestation functionality
- Flexibility, ease of upgrades, and algorithmic changes

The flexibility of FPGAs provides a direct path for changing core algorithms in a hardware device (for example, cryptographic algorithms can be changed, even on the fly) and upgrading software without requiring field replacement of the hardware. Unlike other hardware technologies, the FPGA is field-programmable, giving it an advantage that other technologies lack. For example, when the DES algorithm was broken, any FPGA boards employing the algorithm could have an upgrade installed and the device (with all of the protection and processing benefits of a hardware unit) could continue virtually without interruption. ASIC-based devices, in contrast, cannot be upgraded in this fashion, a particular issue with remote units onboard satellites, for example.

In general, members of the intelligence community operate on the assumption that all cryptographic algorithms will be broken and that they will be replaced at some point in the future. The programmability of the FPGA is a perfect platform for accommodating this eventuality.

Algorithms operate best if they have been optimized. Optimization efforts often continue after initial algorithm deployment, and enhancements can only be realized in the field if the newly optimized algorithm replaces the prior one. Again, FPGAs are perfect for this continual enhancement process.

## SECURITY CONSIDERATIONS

The development of FPGA technology for secure applications requires careful, almost paranoid attention to process integrity. Any lapse in security during the development of the device will create an attack opening that will be all but impossible to close. This begins with the silicon itself. Although FPGAs are usually delivered as a blank slate of unprogrammed cells, care must be taken to assure that the fabricator has not included any back doors or undocumented features (such as "reserved for factory test" PINs or functions) that might be used by an attacker.

Not all FPGAs are the same. When developing a security-sensitive application on an FPGA, the core device must be chosen so that it includes security features that were implemented at the time of manufacture. These should include an encrypted programmable read-only memory (PROM) for volatile devices or the secure version of nonvolatile devices.

The method of storing keys on the device is the next step in building such an application. Keys can be stored either dynamically or statically. Static keys offer the advantage that the boards can be programmed before they are installed on a user's machine. Since static keys are usually not erasable, they can survive power failures or catastrophic interruptions of processes. They do not require battery backups to protect them during such failures or interruptions.

Dynamic keys offer the programmer the ease of erasing and replacing keys, allowing a more dynamic cryptographic environment. Since they require battery backup, failure to monitor and replace batteries at required intervals can result in a variety of problems.

The design of secure applications on an FPGA requires attention to detail with an eye towards attack possibilities. Cross-coupling of IO pins to other critical information-bearing lines within the chip could possibly provide a means for a sophisticated attacker to gain access to cryptographic keys or other secret information. Debug access must be handled carefully so that information regarding secret areas on the chip are not accessible. Even unit power supplies could possibly provide access to sensitive information, and care must be taken to isolate power lines and ground planes from accidentally providing avenues for access. Electromagnetic shielding must be used to minimize probing or at least make it much more difficult.

Open-source code is becoming increasingly popular as a means to achieve faster time to market. But care must be taken that such externally developed code, even if open-source (and therefore subject to external review) is viewed skeptically and carefully for the possible presence of attack avenues.

The development efforts to create modules and designs that will be burned into FPGAs are company jewels that should be treated accordingly. Design reviews, use of version control software, physical protection of the designs and their backups, strict policies governing working from home, and other protection techniques need to be planned in advance and implemented properly.

Management teams should walk through the design area as if they were an attacker intent on stealing the company's secrets—look for easily visible designer PC monitors, unlocked drawers or unprotected PCs overnight or during lunch breaks, passwords written on pieces of paper, etc.

Access to designs should be restricted to a "need to know" basis, and limited to as few key people as possible. Access to files should be logged and (for the more paranoid developers) witnessed and approved.

Designs and software should be encrypted when stored and should require different passwords for different users. Asymmetric-key cryptography with large keys should be used for storing files of any type during the design phase.


**ATTACK VECTORS**

Attackers usually focus on obtaining the cryptographic keys. Since the algorithm being used in any specific application is either public knowledge or can be easily determined by observing characteristics of the encrypted files, obtaining the cryptographic keys are all that stand between an attacker and his ability to compromise a system or masquerade as an authorized user. In one-factor authentication systems, the cryptographic key is often the only thing required to enter a protected environment with no further restraints or limitations.

A less common application that might be encountered by an attacker involves the use of proprietary cryptographic algorithms. In these cases, obtaining the key is necessary but not sufficient. Here the attacker will use the more advanced physical attacks to attempt to obtain both the keys and the algorithm itself. Of course, human engineering (bribes, threats, and subterfuge) can also be employed to obtain the necessary information.

All hardware electronic boards and chips share common threats from physical attack techniques. FPGAs face a particular challenge from physical attacks, since they are based on a well-defined board with known elements that have been altered in known ways to achieve their ultimate function. Unlike a board filled with unknown components that are laid out in unknown ways, the FPGA begins as a clean, regular structure whose layout can be deduced from the settings that are observed in each module.

Attacks on FPGAs generally fall into one of two categories—invasive attacks, which involve a destructive physical attack on the hardware, and noninvasive attacks, which do not destroy the device.

In order to observe the switch settings of the modular structure, the FPGA boards can be subjected to a variety of physical attacks. For example, x-rays can be used to probe the basic content and layout within the board. In the event that a board can be placed in a static state, thermal imaging can be employed to capture a snapshot of the states of components within the circuit while it is in a set state. Sonic probes can provide additional information about the circuit components. A more direct (but time-consuming and costly) approach involves shaving off the top layer of the chip's package and exploring the contents with a scanning electron microscope or other high-resolution probe. Focused-ion-beam probes have also been used to probe the contents of FPGAs.

Computing devices are becoming increasingly mobile. As such, attack vectors through the wireless connectivity channels become the paths of choice. With few exceptions, mobile devices must ultimately employ a standardized communication protocol, such as TCP/IP. Security issues within those protocols become an easy attack path.

It should be noted that such attacks have a point of diminishing returns. The cost of applying progressively more complex attacks increases significantly with the level of security that has been applied in the manufacture of the chip, and the amount of information returned by the probe is only incremental, making the return progressively more costly and less productive. This ultimately results in the attackers turning to other means to obtain the desired information. But the danger to FPGAs due to their structure requires care by the designers of secure applications that will run on them.

**Black-Box Attacks**

Black-box attacks are a technique employed by attackers to attempt to reverse-engineer a board or chip. The concept, as the name implies, is to treat the unit as a black box and change the inputs, developing a truth table of the output, so that patterns can be deduced. For example, if a chip has three inputs and one output, a black-box attack would systematically enter stimuli and observe the output. Such a study might appear as shown in Table 9.1.

**Table 9.1**    A black-box truth table.

| Inputs | | | Output |
|---|---|---|---|
| A | B | C | D (A,B,C) |
| 0 | 0 | 0 | 0 |
| 0 | 0 | 1 | 0 |
| 0 | 1 | 0 | 0 |
| 0 | 1 | 1 | 1 |
| 1 | 0 | 0 | 0 |
| 1 | 0 | 1 | 1 |
| 1 | 1 | 0 | 1 |
| 1 | 1 | 1 | 1 |

In this simple example, a single stimulus is changed and both the stimulus and the output are recorded in a truth table. This process can be used in conjunction with a Karnaugh-table process to determine some information about the logic contents of the black box. Of course the complexity of this process grows exponentially with the number of inputs and so is best applied only to the most elemental component of a target logic circuit.

**Readback Attacks**

Most FPGA circuits provide a readback feature. This allows the programmer to read out the configuration of the FPGA to enable faster debugging during the development and testing cycles. The readback attack (see Dipert[1]) employs this feature through the programming interface to obtain information about the contents and configuration of the FPGA (such as cryptographic keys and algorithms). This functionality can usually be disabled by the programmer by using one or more specific bits dedicated to turning the readback functionality off. It is important that this feature be disabled in order to provide some protection against the attack.

With every precaution come ways to break it. Boneh et al.[2] used fault injection to overcome the protection against readback attacks. They showed how to use the technique to break asymmetric-key cryptography such as the Rabin and RSA schemes by using hardware-induced faults. Fault injection can be accomplished through a variety of means that have been successfully demonstrated, including electromagnetic radiation (Quisqauter et al.[3]), infrared laser light (Ajluni[4]), and a flash of incoherent light (Skorobogatov and Anderson[5]). A complementary work by Biham and Shamir[6] introduced an analysis technique that can be applied to symmetric-key-cryptography algorithms. Although the research articles report the use of the techniques on ASICs, there is no reason to believe that they would not work on FPGAs as well. Using these techniques, one can override the security bits that disable the readback function, allowing the attacker to use the function to gain information about the configuration of the FPGA.

## SRAM FPGAs

Some implementations of applications employ static random-access memory (SRAM) in conjunction with an FPGA. In these, the configuration data is stored unprotected in the SRAM outside of the FPGA, and the developers rely upon the volatile nature of SRAMs to "forget" the information on power-down. If the configuration data is stored in PROMs and then loaded into the device during power-up, an attack would likely focus on the communication between the PROM and the device.

Unfortunately, SRAM FPGAs do not entirely lose the information stored within on power-down. Gutmann[7] showed that fundamental transport mechanisms (including electromigration, hot carriers, and ionic contamination) within semiconductors actually create residual images of the data that are retained after power-down. These residual images can be read long after the device has lost power. One example of data recovery was reported by Anderson et al.[8], in which the cryptographic key was recovered from a module that had been used by a bank. Since the device had employed the same key for a long period of time, the image of the key had been burned into the SRAM by electromigration, and the image could be read even after power had been turned off. Given these and other results, it appears that physical attacks against SRAM FPGAs can be successful.

## Antifuse FPGAs

Antifuse FPGAs (AF FPGAs) employ a thin insulating layer between conductors. The device is programmed by applying a voltage across the insulator, which then becomes a low-resistance conductor. This is effectively a small, 100-nanometer connection between the conductors. The programming is permanent once this change has been applied. Studies have shown that, although it is feasible to determine the programming by physically probing the layers to locate the modified insulator, the process is destructive, time-consuming, and expensive. It is not considered to be a practical attack path.

## Flash FPGAs

Another FPGA approach employs flash transistors (used in flash memory) as the programming mechanism. The gain of the connecting transistors changes once they have been programmed. Unlike other FPGA programming approaches, this approach leaves no optical signature (such as a burned connection) for detection by attackers. However, the transistors do emit various forms of emissions while operating that can be detected by electron microscopes and other technologies. In order to do this, the attacker must be able to get an electron beam into the chip's chambers, which requires removal of packaging and possible sectioning to remove cover layers. There is some debate as to how practical, difficult, or expensive this might be.

One of the limitations of flash technology is the finite number of read/write cycles that can be performed before the device begins to fail. Many reads can cause buildup of charge, causing the flash transistor's operating point to change. This ultimately causes the connection to fail. Moreover, changing the gain characteristics of the transistor is achieved by migrating charges across the junction during the programming step. One of the characteristics of semiconductors is that charges will migrate away from one another over time, causing the transistor's gain properties to slowly decay back to their basic state. It might be possible for an attacker to exploit these properties, but no successful such experiments have been published to date.

## Indirect Attacks

Since FPGAs consume power, there may be additional, perhaps nonobvious, channels by which an attacker can obtain information about secrets that are stored on the device. Power consumption can be subjected to power analysis to determine if power drawn by various chips during the transmission or storing of ones and zeros that comprise a key might be reflected on the power line to the board. Kocher et al.[9] introduced two attacks that work using power-consumption analysis—simple power analysis and differential power analysis. The authors were able to find the secret keys on a tamper resistant device using these techniques without any prior knowledge of the structure of the device. Building on these approaches, other researchers have been able to improve upon the techniques and have also successfully used electromagnetic emissions (analyzed in a similar fashion) to obtain stored secrets.

## PREVENTING ATTACKS

As explained above, black-box attacks become exponentially more difficult to execute due to the increasing complexity of FPGA devices. These are not generally viewed as practical in the intelligence community. In fact, building on this point, it is possible to establish some rules of thumb that can be used as guides to developers of secure FPGA devices.

Retention effects due to charge migration and related processes can be best avoided by either inverting the data periodically (recording the current polarity with a state bit) or moving data around. Measured time constants beyond which measurable retention effects begin to appear are approximately 500 seconds, so this movement should be completed once every few minutes.

Propagating data repeatedly down the same paths can also create retention effects. This can be avoided by moving the location of the circuitry that will perform the repetitive operations (not particularly practical) or by adding some "erasing" random data whose cycles are ignored by the circuitry. Erasing of secret-bearing cells should be performed with repetitive erase/write cycles that randomize any residual effects from the presence of the stored data.

Approaches to the prevention of attacks on FPGAs fall into either the software or hardware categories. Due to their flexibility and ease of deployment, software approaches tend to dominate the prevention field. Software approaches generally involve the use of random noise added to cells or data and then separated out in subsequent steps. Hardware approaches usually focus on removing data signatures from power pins and reducing emissions from transistors.

## REFERENCES

[1] Dipert, B., "Cunning circuits confound crooks," 2000. Available at http://www.e-insite.net/ednmag/contents/images/21df2.pdf.
[2] Boneh, D., DeMillo, R. A., and Lipton, R. J., "On the Importance of Checking Cryptographic Protocols for Faults (Extended Abstract)," in W. Fumy, ed., *Advances in Cryptology-EUROCRYPT '97*, Vol. LNCS 1233, 1997, Springer-Verlag, pp. 37–51.

3 Quisquater, J. J. and Samyde, D., "Electro Magnetic Analysis (EMA): Measures and Countermeasures for Smart Cards," In *International Conference on Research in Smart Cards*, E-smart, 2001, Cannes, France, pp. 200–210.

4 Ajluni, C., "Two New Imaging Techniques to Improve IC Defect Indentication," in *Electronic Design* 43, 1995, 14 (July), pp. 37–38.

5 Skorobogatov, S. and Anderson, R., "Optical Fault Induction Attacks," in, B. S. Kaliski, Jr., C., K. Ko,c, and C. Paar, eds., *Workshop on Cryptographic Hardware and Embedded Systems—CHES* 2002, Vol. LNCS 2523. Springer-Verlag, pp. 2–12.

6 Biham, E. and Shamir, A., "Differential Fault Analysis of Secret Key Cryptosystems," in B. Kaliski, Jr., ed., *Advances in Cryptology, CRYPTO '97* Vol. LNCS 1294, Springer-Verlag, pp. 513–525.

7 Gutmann, P., "Data Permanence in Semiconductor Devices," in *10th USENIX Security Symposium*, 2001, pp. 39–54.

8 Anderson, R. and Kuhn, M., "Low Cost Attacks on Tamper Resistant Devices," in B. Christianson, B. Crispo, T. M. A. Lomas, and M. Roe, eds., *5th International Workshop on Security Protocols*, Vol. LNCS 1361, 1997, Springer-Verlag, pp. 125–136.

9 Kocher, P., Jaffe, J., and Jun, B., "Differential Power Analysis," in M. Wiener, ed., *Advances in Cryptology, CRYPTO '99*, Vol. LNCS 1666, 1999, Springer-Verlag, pp. 388–397.

# Chapter 10

## HARDWARE-BASED AUTHENTICATION

### WHO IS AT THE OTHER END?

The remoteness of people and devices on networks is at once their strength and their weakness. If one can ascertain (with complete confidence) the identity of the person or device at the other end of the communication, then the link provides a means to transcend the limits of space and conduct business across arbitrary distances. But the operative phrase is "with complete confidence." The process of establishing the identity of a remote party with high (or, ideally, complete) confidence is called authentication. It can occur between people, devices, or any combination thereof.

There are three classes of authentication that we will consider in this chapter:

- Authentication of a person
- Authentication of a device
- Authentication of the physical environment around either the person or the device

As explained in previous chapters, many systems have been developed over the years that employ various forms of trust protected or validated by encryption. Such systems ultimately depend on a root basis of the trust, and any compromise to that root, at either end of any authentication process, can cause the confidence in or validity of the trust to erode rapidly. There are various hardware and software means that can be employed to protect the chain of trust, but all of these assume that the root of trust is valid.

Previous chapters have explored various methods to establish and protect this root trust in devices. The remainder of this book will deal with technologies that seek to authenticate people or some aspect of the person. Some of these technologies can be applied to further authenticate devices as well, and these will be identified.

## AUTHENTICATION OF A PERSON

The idea that it is possible to identify a person with complete certainty arises from commonly held beliefs (such as the belief that each person's fingerprint or DNA is unique) combined with personal experience (few people have ever encountered a stranger whom they completely believed was a close friend or relative). Although there may be some degree of truth to the notions that DNA and fingerprints are largely unique, the fact is that a great deal of uncertainty is introduced into the process of measuring these fingerprints, DNA, or any other biometric. This uncertainty makes the occurrence of a false positive (an impersonator using his own fingerprint on someone else's fingerprint reader and gaining access) not infrequent.

Biometric devices are used for one of two purposes: to verify that a user is genuine (by comparing his biometric measurement against the measurements of the claimed identity) or to identify a person (by comparing his biometric data to a database of many measurements of many different people). It is common knowledge that humans use a variety of bodily characteristics (face, body, voice, manner of walking) to recognize one another. Lab studies have shown that animals use the same basic measurements to recognize their family members. Biometric technologies have been developed to capture one or another of those characteristics in a unique and reproducible way in order to enable verification and identification. But none of these devices is perfect.

Biometric systems have four basic elements. They include a sensor, which captures the biometric data, some feature-extraction software, a software module that performs basic matching functions, and a decision module.

### Enrollment

The optimal performance of any biometric system depends upon a proper capture of the genuine user's biometric characteristics at the time he is enrolled into the system. Failure to do so will skew the behavior of the system. For example, if a user places his finger to one side of a biometric scanner during enrollment, the system will best recognize the user's fingerprint when he again places it to the side. The enrollment process should use several different captures of the user's biometric in order to store a range of possible conditions that might be subsequently encountered when the user is presenting his biometric for recognition. These are typically stored in a secure user database.

### Recognition

Once a user has been enrolled in the system, he can present his biometric in "real world" conditions for recognition by the system. It is important to define the metrics that describe biometric technology and its ability to recognize a user. Independent of the type of biometric-sensing technology being used, natural variations occur. With fingerprint readers, for example, a user may not place his finger in a good position. Dirt might alter the optical quality of the scan. Cuts, oils, or grease on the finger may alter the measurements. The user might apply varying amounts of pressure during successive scans, thereby squeezing the whorls of the fingerprint more or less from measurement to measurement. Environmental characteristics might alter the finger, the optics, or the electronics. Other biometric devices might suffer from sensitivities to other parameters. In fact, the probability that a user's characteristics will yield exactly the same measurements in two successive scans is nearly zero. But in the final analysis, there is no perfect biometric sensor at this time. Noise in the measurement process, due either to the device or variations in the capture process, overwhelms the theoretical uniqueness of any biometric technology.

There are varying degrees of recognition provided by sensors, measured by their false acceptance or false rejection rates. In order to provide a degree of reliability to such noisy systems, a scan is assigned a *similarity score* which can be directly translated to the degree of confidence that the user presenting the fingerprint (for example) is the user whose characteristics are being compared against in a database. The higher the score, the higher the confidence that the two fingerprints match. In operation, the system administrator sets a threshold t. If the similarity score s meets or exceeds the threshold t, the user's fingerprint is declared a match against the comparison being examined in the database. If the similarity score s is below the threshold t, the system declares that this is a different person than the one in the database.

Over time, data is collected from a variety of persons declared "different." The distribution of these scores is called an "impostor distribution." By the same process, the distribution of scores generated by measurements in which the user is declared to be a match is called the "genuine distribution."

A biometric device is typically characterized by its error rate. There are two basic error rates that are important:

- False rejection rate (FRR): the rate at which biometric measurements from the same person are declared to be different
- False acceptance rate (FAR): the rate at which the device declares an impostor to be the genuine person.

Of course, the FRR and FAR are direct functions of the threshold. Lower thresholds will produce more false matches and fewer false non-matches. If the system is operating in a highly variable (noisy) environment where there is a great deal of variability in successive measurements of a genuine user, operators might be tempted to make the threshold lower. But this makes the system less secure, since more false matches will occur. If high security is desired, there will be fewer false matches, but more false non-matches—genuine users will need to understand that it might take multiple attempts before they are recognized.

In general, impostor and genuine user scores show Gaussian distributions. It is not possible to draw a Gaussian distribution accurately. Gaussians have infinite extent—the probability decreases with distance from the peak of the distribution but never truly reaches zero. As a result,

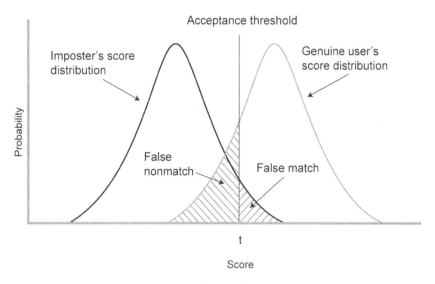

**Figure 10.1**  Biometric error rates.

no biometric system that displays randomness in measurements will ever completely separate impostors from genuine users. There will always be an FAR as well as an FRR.

As can be seen from Figure 10.1, the threshold t determines the area of intersection between the two Gaussians above and below t. Those impostor scores that exceed t will be accepted as genuine, and those genuine user scores that are below t will be rejected as false. Setting the threshold higher reduces the false acceptances but increases the false rejections. The setting is determined by the nature of the information being protected and the tolerance of genuine users to being rejected. In general, high-security situations employ higher thresholds, and civilian applications employ thresholds that are centered between the two distributions. Better biometric technologies will have narrow distributions whose peaks are widely separated, leaving small areas for FAR and FRR.

### The Use of Multiple Biometrics

Some organizations employ more than one biometric in an additive fashion before granting access to a user. In this mode, the user's first biometric (such as a fingerprint) must be recognized and his second, independent biometric (such as an iris scan or the print of a different finger) must also be recognized. This reduces the overall FAR (thereby creating a more secure environment) but increases the FRR (thereby increasing the number of tries a genuine user will have to complete before gaining access). Administrators must decide a proper balance between these two until such time that biometric measurements themselves are more reliable and less prone to errors.

## COMMON BIOMETRIC TECHNOLOGIES

### Signature

The use of a signature dates back to the beginning of the use of the written word. People used to authenticate documents with their mark, made in any of a number of ways, such as through the use of sealing wax or through the use of a special mark that the genuine user made with his pen, knife, or other indelible instrument. This evolved into a user's personal signature, usually pen and ink to paper, which is still employed today to execute or witness legal documents in the presence of independent witnesses.

People with an ability to copy someone else's signature began to intervene in the process, usually for the purposes of theft. Forgeries made by professionals were used to steal money from bank accounts of victims, possibly because the banks may have only used a cursory confirmation of the signature.

In the digital world, an effort to introduce the equivalent of a signed document was made in 1988 with the development of the X.509 certificate. In a PKI implementation, a user is registered with a certifying authority (CA). The CA is bound by law to take appropriate measures to independently assure the user's authenticity. The CA is a third party, without affiliations to other companies. Once the CA has registered a user, an asymmetric-key pair is generated by the user and the public key posted freely on the CA site and any other locations the user wishes. When digitally signing a document, the user employs his private key to create a digital certificate that includes a hash summary of the document at the time of signing. The hash summary is encrypted using the user's private key, and any outside party can view the digital certificate by using the user's public key. Any alteration to the document will be immediately detected by the decryption process, and the document will be flagged as invalid.

The security pivot point of digital signatures is the root of trust that is established during the issuance of the initial certificate by the CA. If there is any failure to properly establish the authenticity of the user, the system will lose its trustworthiness. Such failures can lead to the creation of false identities who can "attest" to the legitimacy of documents by signing them without the knowledge of recipients who are trusting the signature (much like a forgery in the physical world). The system relies upon trust.

## Face

Face recognition is used in both the human and animal kingdoms to recognize someone who is known. The method by which humans recognize faces is complex and the subject of much research. It is more robust than face-recognition algorithms that are currently available, since humans can recognize others independent of lighting, the viewing perspective, and sometimes even without regard to the effects of age. The use of facial recognition in the animal kingdom has been verified by a variety of carefully conducted psychology tests whose results were subject to peer review.

Every face has many features that are common to all but that vary from person to person. Separation of the eyes, width of the nose, shape of the cheekbones, positions of the ears with respect to other features, and measurements of jawbone length are just a few examples of such features. In all, the average human face has some 80 fixed points that can be used by an algorithm to characterize it as a biometric. Measurements of distances between these 80 points are accumulated into a *faceprint* that can then be stored in a database.

Capture of a user's face for proper recognition is subject to a variety of factors. Low or high light levels can cause problems with under- or over-exposure, often resulting in the inability to capture some of the fixed points that are needed by the recognition algorithm. Orientation of the person can also cause the camera to be unable to acquire specific required features. The presence of hats, glasses, and makeup can disrupt the measurement process. Distance of user from the camera, when combined with the magnification of the imaging optics, can reduce the number of pixels that are employed in the capture of the user's image. This reduces the accuracy of the recognition algorithm, causing increased FARs and FRRs. When employed in real-world situations (such as on busy streets or in airport terminals), facial-recognition technology still requires further improvement before these rates reach acceptable levels.

## Gait

People have individual styles of walking based on their musculoskeletal system, their mood, and other factors. Although it is known that a person's gait is used (along with face and body recognition) to help someone identify another, the implementation of gait as a biometric technology has not yet made sufficient strides to allow its use as a reliable form of biometric technology.

### Keystroke Timing

When a person types a specific string of characters such as those that comprise a pass phrase, the time that he keeps his finger on a key and the time between successive keystrokes can be measured as a function of the character being typed within the string. These two factors can then be averaged over multiple instances that are acquired during the enrollment process to build a statistical average that can be used as a signature for the person. Research in this field began in approximately 1980 and has improved the technology and its reliability over time. Studies such as those performed by Monrose and Rubin[1] and Mahar et al.[2] demonstrate that these signatures are reasonably stable and unique to each person. This *keystroke-timing* biometric uses no extra hardware but rather utilizes the existing keyboard to develop a profile for a specific user that is later used to verify a user's authenticity. Keystroke-timing systems often employ a neural network or a Bayesian filter that "learns" a person's signature characteristics during the enrollment process and uses this during a later comparison step to develop a score for the degree of match. A clip level is set, above which the person is deemed to have been authenticated.

With the increase in mobile computing, users today often find themselves at more than one device with its own unique keyboard—in this case the enrollment process must be repeated for each keyboard and the keystroke-timing signature stored locally. Use of the technology for remote login would require multiple stored profiles for each user, one for each keyboard.

### Fingerprint

Fingerprints have been in use for centuries as a means of uniquely identifying people. The patterns of loops and whorls for a specific finger can be captured by an imprint of some form (ink, wax, clay, etc.) and used as the basis for later comparison to fingerprints captured under different circumstances. Even though fingerprints have been in use for such a long time and millions of fingerprints have been amassed into various databases, matching fingerprints from two different individuals have never been found. Although this is far from conclusive (and not by any means mathematically rigorous), this is often cited as justification for the assertion that no two people on earth have the same fingerprints. The digital world makes the process of capture and storage much cleaner, more reliable, and more transportable. When a person places his finger on a compact fingerprint-scanning device, it captures digital images of the fingerprint. The image can then be analyzed for features that might be unique to the person and compared to either a local database (for verification) that controls access to information (such as a room or a PC's files) or to a remote database (for identification) that contains similarly processed features of many other individuals.

There are several different core technologies that are used in fingerprint readers. They include:

- Optical scanners (both two- and three-dimensional)
- Capacitive sensors
- Thermal sensors
- Ultrasonic sensors
- Electric field sensors

The first two classes, optical and capacitive, dominate fingerprint-scanning products and will be examined in more depth in a subsequent chapter. The cost of these devices is often $20 or less, and two-dimensional scanners can be small enough to be integrated into a flash drive or laptop.

Some optical fingerprint scanners employ two-dimensional imaging, which allows very compact, flat sensors that can easily be integrated into flash drives and laptops. However, since the scan is restricted to two dimensions, there are concerns that high-quality digital photographic prints of a user's finger may allow a false acceptance, thereby allowing an attacker to gain access. These concerns are addressed by three-dimensional scanners, in which a more complex set of optics is combined with an imaging device to both obtain the two-dimensional image and also extract features that are only present if a three-dimensional finger is present on the device's surface at the time of scanning. By looking for the heights of ridges in the fingerprint as well as distances between specific features, such devices gather more information about a person's fingerprint, thereby reducing false acceptances and detecting simple attempts to present images of fingerprints.

In spite of the extra geometric requirements placed by optics on a fingerprint, three-dimensional detectors have also been defeated. In these cases, attackers carefully created a wax or rubber imprint of a user's finger and then used a simple casting process to construct a reasonable recreation of the user's finger in three dimensions (such as in silicone rubber or gelatin). The use of such a fake finger allowed a measurable increase in the FAR of the reader.

### Voiceprint

*Voiceprint* technology (also called *voice recognition*) uses specific features in a person's speech to determine who is speaking (as opposed to *speech recognition*, which seeks to determine what is being said independent of the speaker). The term "voiceprint" unfortunately gives a misleading impression that, like a fingerprint, a person's voice has fixed and unique characteristics. In actual fact, these characteristics can change due to a person's stress or physical health. Moreover, a voiceprint is actually a spectrum (rather than a "print" in any sense) of a person's voice that is then subjected to various forms of analysis.

It has been shown in various laboratory studies that acoustic patterns reflect a specific user's anatomical structure (the shape of the mouth and throat) and speaking style (the user's pitch, accent, and speech patterns). The quantification of these characteristics can be used to create a form of template for the user against which subsequent words or phrases can be compared to determine the degree of match. In order to accomplish this quantification, voiceprint systems employ different techniques, such as:

- Frequency estimation, in which the frequency or power spectrum of the user's voice when he speaks a certain word or phrase is captured and used as a template
- Neural networks, in which systems of artificial neurons and pathways "learn" to recognize features within the user's speech spectrum
- Hidden Markov models, in which patterns are "learned" as more and more samples of a user's speech are presented to the device during an enrollment phase
- Matrix representations, in which the correlation strengths among different factors are built up during the enrollment phase and later used as a template for recognition

In all of these cases, the system must proceed through two phases—an enrollment or training phase, in which the user speaks certain requested sentences and phrases, and a test phase, in which the specific recognition algorithm (above) is used to attempt to recognize the user's speech. Low scores usually indicate a need for additional training.

In order to optimize the recognition process, voice-recognition systems usually ask the user to speak a pass phrase during the training and testing process. The same pass phrase is then used later during the recognition or verification process. Like a pass phrase that is entered by a user on a keyboard while seeking entry into a computer system, the voice pass phrase adds the advantage that an attacker must know the precise pass phrase that the target user employed during the training process. Armed with this information, the attacker must then also produce a recognizable reproduction of the target user's speech characteristics, a difficult task at best unless a digital recorder is used.

To add complexity to the pass-phrase concept, systems have added a multiplicity of pass phrases for each user during the enrollment process. During the recognition/verification step, the user is asked to repeat a pass phrase selected at random. By constructing the pass phrases so that they are answers to specific questions (such as "what is your mother's maiden name?"), such systems can make the voice-recognition process more impervious to attackers without making it more difficult to use. Tape-recorder attacks would be further prevented by adding timeouts after the question is asked to eliminate situations where attackers skip forward or back to different recorded answers.

Alternative implementations involve the use of prompted text that the user is asked to read during the training session. In this case, the voice-recognition algorithms are much more complex, since they must extract specific information from a much broader "template" of speech elements. This enrollment process can be used as part of a text-prompted system, in which the user is asked to speak text that is presented on a screen, or on a text-independent system, in which the user can speak anything he wishes. In the latter case, the user's cooperation (or even knowledge of the voice-recognition process) is required. It is the most versatile but also the most demanding of the recognition algorithms.

Noise can affect the FAR and FRR numbers of voice-recognition technology. In some cases, the technology is used as part of a two-factor authentication system, combining it with an RFID, a smart card, or a biometric in order to decrease the FAR and FRR numbers. Other systems continually "learn" from the user's current submitted speech sample, adjusting it over time.

**Retinal Scan**

The retinal scan is a biometric technology that measures the pattern of blood vessels in the back (on the retina) of a person's eye. First used in the

1930s, the technology uses a low-level light source to illuminate the retinal pattern of blood vessels and project it through the eye's lens back onto a detector. The captured image can then be analyzed and recorded. The user must remove his glasses in order to use the system and then focus his vision on a certain point in order to hold the eye steady during capture.

A person's retina is unique to that person and remains stable throughout his lifetime. To date there is no known way to create a "fake" retina, and the small blood vessels in the back of the eye decay very quickly in a dead person, making the use of his eye (as seen in movies) impossible. These features, combined with the high accuracy (very low FAR and FRR numbers), make the technology appealing to very high-security establishments. Its cost and difficulty of use do not make it appealing for broad consumer applications.

## Iris Scan

The iris is the colored ring in the eye between the white portion (the sclera) and the pupil (the small, dark aperture). The structures and features seen in the iris form during pregnancy and stabilize within two years or so after birth. The uniqueness, variety, and stability of the features in the iris promise very low FAR and FRR numbers. Like fingerprints, iris patterns are different even for identical twins, and there is no known way to create a fake iris (contact lenses are easily detected) or otherwise alter anyone's iris. These features, combined with the speed and accuracy of recognition, indicate that the technology may be a significant player in future biometric implementations if ease of use and cost concerns can be addressed.

## Palm Print

Palm-print biometric methods employ the same technologies that are used in fingerprint biometrics. Like a finger, a person's palm has a unique pattern of friction ridges and whorls on the surface of the skin. An optical scanner captures a two- or three-dimensional picture of these patterns and stores them for later analysis and use in a recognition process. The scanner is much larger than that employed in a fingerprint scanner, and much more data is captured. Due to the significantly larger amount of data, palm prints generally have lower FAR and FRR numbers, thereby providing a more reliable authentication process. The sensor technologies used for palm prints are the same as those used in fingerprint scanners.

## Hand Geometry

An additional approach to biometric authentication of a person is the use of hand geometry as a unique signature. Using a hand-sized device, this technology measures a number of features of the hand, including shape, size of the palm, lengths of the various digits within each finger, and their respective widths. The technology is largely unaffected by humidity or temperature. It is of course affected by growth (the hand-geometry measurements of children and adolescents continue to change during growth). Rings have been known to affect the operation of hand geometry readers, as do changes in the shape of the hand due to arthritis.

The fundamentally limited number of hand measurements available to the technology impacts the uniqueness of the signature. That is, the likelihood of another person having the same measurements is quite high. Therefore, the technology is best used for verification only rather than identification. Moreover, there are security concerns about its high FAR. The technology is not generally used for higher-security applications. The large size of the reader generally eliminates it from consideration for use in laptops.

### Infrared Thermogram

The human body radiates heat approximately equivalent to a 100-watt light bulb. The specific distribution of the radiated heat is specific to each person and can be captured by a digital camera operating in the infrared. This *thermogram* signature is non-invasive (a remote camera can capture the image). Some implementations do not capture the entire body thermogram but rather employ the heat radiated by the back of a clenched fist to determine the vein structure underneath the skin.

The technology is limited by two factors—its high cost (infrared digital cameras are expensive) and its susceptibility to environmental influences. In the latter limitation, uncontrolled heat sources such as an incandescent bulb, the presence of other people within the field of view of the infrared camera, and heating ducts in the background can all make the extraction of a person's thermogram difficult.

### DNA

At the very root of human individuality is our DNA—deoxyribonucleic acid. This one-dimensional, double-helix code of organic molecules contains the blueprint for constructing a complete person. Each person's DNA is unique, unless they have one twin (or more in the case of triplets, etc.). In the case of identical twins, each twin's DNA is identical to the DNA of the other twin. DNA testing is usually performed by comparing the DNA signature of a person to a known sample collected from the person under test conditions. The control sample must have been stored under high-security conditions to avoid tampering or replacement with alternate

DNA. DNA testing is most often used today for forensics. It is generally considered one of the most reliable means of authenticating a person's identity.

Unlike concepts presented in movies or action novels, DNA as a biometric is far from practical at this time. DNA typing uses wet chemistry that requires an expert's talents. It is a complex process that can often take two weeks or longer before a result is obtained. Moreover, the accuracy of DNA testing is good to only 0.001 percent, or one part in 100,000.

Two other concerns inhibit the practicality of this technology as a biometric. First, contamination of a sample is relatively easy. Anyone's DNA sample can replace an authenticated user's sample, thereby allowing a subversion of the system. User samples can be obtained without their knowledge by careful scouring of a person's workplace for skin or hair samples that fall regularly. Second, there are serious privacy issues that arise with the technology. DNA samples not only can be used to authenticate a user but also to identify certain diseases and other genetic defects. Information about these conditions could be used against a person in discrimination or other illegal practices. At this time, DNA sampling as a biometric technology is not practical or safe. More development is required.

## AUTHENTICATION OF A DEVICE

Just as it is important to know who a user is, it is also important in some circumstances to know with what device one is communicating. Many manufacturers have added device identification numbers (*device ID*) to the hardware unit, typically burned into a location that is not alterable after burning. Others take additional steps to employ encryption and tamper evidence to protect the device ID, such as in the case of TPM devices. These steps are designed to prevent easy cloning of mission-critical devices.

Device authentication usually operates in a challenge/response fashion—a command is issued from an application, demanding that the device identify itself. The device then returns its identification number, either in open-text form, encrypted, or as a hash summary. The requesting application then compares it to what was expected and notifies the user of any anomalies. (For examples, see Chapter 8 on TPM technology.) A recent development using clock skew as a fingerprint is described in a subsequent section in this chapter.

There are groups of users, such as the Electronic Freedom Foundation, that have raised concerns about user privacy vis â vis the use of device authentication. They express the concern that the use of a device identification number, or several from the same PC, could easily lead to the identification of the user himself without necessarily notifying him or otherwise asking his permission. There is also a concern that device IDs could be used as a means to exclude competitors from using their hardware in particular machines or on specified operating systems. Moreover, device IDs might impact the ability of virtualization applications to operate smoothly on remote devices. It is argued that uniformity among all types of devices will encourage the propagation of virtualization applications. System administrators will need to decide which of these represents the higher priority—device authentication or user privacy.

## AUTHENTICATION OF THE SURROUNDING ENVIRONMENT

Location is quickly becoming an important element of the authentication process. In certain high-security environments, users need to be granted access to information based on their roles and privileges, the device upon which they are operating, and their current specific location. For example, a conference room might be deemed secure enough for executives of a company to gain access to corporate financial information before it is released to the public. In this case, it is necessary to require not only that the user and his PC be authenticated but also his current location. (Perhaps corporate policy precludes anyone examining such information over a wireless connection while he has coffee in a shop down the street.)

Delivery of information can also be tied to an authenticated location, and various technologies have appeared that sense a device's location in order to control access.

### Wi-Fi Hotspot

Wireless access points are becoming increasingly common, often with installations in user homes. In buildings that have one or more businesses, the presence of multiple access points is very common. The principle behind the use of a group of wireless access points to determine the location of a wireless-enabled computer (such as a laptop) is to use the relative signal strengths of surrounding known access points to determine approximate location. The system does not require actually being connected to any of the access points but rather uses the relative signal strengths of the access points, combined with some prior knowledge of the physical location of those access points, to make a determination of the laptop's physical location. Another advantage of the approach is that an administrator can sit in his office with a map of the locations of the wireless access points within the building to create the database that the software needs to infer location.

Issues facing the technology include the ease with which access points can be moved or spoofed, concerns about access points being present or absent at any given time (due to owners turning them off), and the unexpected appearance of new access points.

### IP address

Fixed IP addresses are assigned to hosts (typically Internet service providers) who then can use Dynamic host configuration protocol (DHCP) technology to assign non-permanent IP addresses to computers that log into its domain. Since the physical location of the host is known at the time the fixed IP address is obtained, it is a simple matter to assume that anyone attached to the host is physically nearby. This is actually not a good assumption, but it's a first guess. Beyond that, recording of the trail of intermediate IP addresses that data packets experience between the actual computer and the host can be used to further refine knowledge of the PC's location. The IP address is considered a very crude approximation of the user's location. The use of a local-area network (LAN) within a business can further constrain IP addresses, but even here technologies such as virtual private networks (VPNs) can be used to connect remotely to a LAN and obtain a local IP address, thereby losing the location information that might otherwise have been obtained. The use of IP address for location authentication is not considered reliable and should be used with caution.

### Clock Skew

An approach developed and reported by Kohno et al.[3] uses microscopic deviations in device hardware that vary from PC to PC. These deviations are called *clock skew* and seem to provide a unique device fingerprint for any specific PC. Kohno et al. report that the clock skew maintains its signature characteristics over thousands of miles of packet transmission, independent of where or how the device is connected to the Internet. It is not masked by firewalls or network address translators and cannot be masked by sites that claim to provide a degree of anonymity to a user. The use of network time protocol to adjust the local clock, or satellite sources such as GPS, does not affect the clock-skew signature. Although an excellent method to fingerprint a specific device, the technology does not add any information about location. However, its value as a device fingerprint stands on its own merits.

## GPS

The *global positioning system* (GPS) uses the relative arrival time of synchronized timing pulses received from multiple satellites to determine a device's physical location on the surface of the earth. Using knowledge of the current satellite positions in their orbits, along with the satellite signature embedded with each timing signal, the system can produce geolocation information with accuracies of 10 feet or so, depending on the surrounding environment. GPS technology is rapidly expanding as the list of user applications for driving directions, marking of hiking trails, surveying, search and rescue, and others continues to grow.

Although very intuitive and easily integrated with mapping applications to pinpoint a location, the technology has several fundamental limitations that reduce its value for location authentication. The GPS timing signals are weak, requiring advanced weak-signal detection techniques and mathematical correlators to obtain a lock on a timing signal from any given satellite. The presence of RF noise at 1.2 or 1.5 GHz can cause a device to either lose lock or render it unable to capture lock in the first place. The GPS signals are reflected by buildings, the ground, and other environmental objects, adding additional confusion to the mathematics of determining geolocation in urban areas. Moreover, these buildings and the earth's ionosphere can attenuate and disperse the signals as a function of frequency, acting much like a refractive medium, further complicating the calculation and adding uncertainty and noise. Jamming units can easily be constructed to flood the GPS portion of the spectrum with white noise, which renders GPS receivers incapable of obtaining or maintaining lock. GPS generators, used by manufacturers for testing purposes, emit a set of very strong timing signals that duplicates a false constellation of satellites, thereby causing any GPS receivers in the vicinity (this can be miles) to alter its location calculation to reflect whatever the generator has elected to emit. This effectively spoofs a receiver's location.

By itself, GPS is considered one of several possible components of a location-authentication system but cannot be relied upon alone for high-security applications.

## Radio-Frequency Measurements

There are currently two classes of radio-frequency (RF) measurements that are being employed for location authentication: radio-frequency spectrum measurements and location fingerprints using the RF.

### Radio-Frequency Spectrum

In any given location, electronic equipment that is operating emits radio waves that contribute to the overall frequency spectrum. The strength of different components at different frequencies depends on the distance between the receiver and the source as well as the source strength and its particular distribution of waves across frequencies. In principle, this could be used to create an RF fingerprint for a given location. Unlike GPS, such a fingerprint would not provide geolocation, just something that can be recognized if it is present.

There are problems with this type of approach. A PC's lights, wireless access points, etc., are turned on and off at arbitrary times of day. Each such action changes the RF spectrum. Moreover, once such an RF spectrum is captured, even by a brief visit to the space with a broad-spectrum receiver, the spectrum can be easily duplicated. The technology as it currently exists is not sufficiently stable to be used as a location signature.

### Location Fingerprints

A novel location fingerprint technology that has been developed and deployed by Digital Authentication Technologies, Inc., takes advantage of the fact that remote timing signals from distant sources pick up delays due to intervening free electrons and dielectric materials. By using knowledge of the direction of a specific remote timing source, dielectric content in a specific direction can be measured. This is further augmented by using a mixture of various timing sources that provide scanning of the hemisphere about a location. This full process makes it possible to characterize the stable substructure of dielectrics about a point and, to the extent that this substructure is stable, recognize that characterization at a future time. Studies to date in both lab and field tests show that such characterizations have a spatial resolution of about 10-20 feet and are stable over years. The technology is not easily subject to spoofing, since such a task would require altering the dielectric content surrounding a location in a manner that is not detected by the user or the administrator. Moreover, the RF processing has also been used as an RNG (without using any algorithm) that can produce keys of arbitrary lengths with no measurable patterns or initialization conditions. Previously measured dielectric RF signals at a target location are not sufficient to create a faked location credential, since the server also knows the current time and RF signal source positions at the subject's location. Previously captured RF signals will display the wrong positional information for that time, and so spoofed data can be detected. Moreover, the use of deep historical tables of these RF numbers on both the client and server sides eliminates replay attacks.

## REFERENCES

[1] Fabian Monrose and Aviel Rubin, "Authentication via keystroke dynamics," *Fourth ACM Conference on Computer and Communications Security*, 1997, pp. 48–56, 1997.

[2] D. Mahar, R. Napier, M. Wagner, W. Laverty, R. Henderson, and M. Hiron, "Optimizing digraph-latency based biometric typist verification systems: inter and intra typist differences in digraph latency distributions," *Int. Journal of Human-Computer Studies*, 43, 1995, pp. 579–592, 1995.

[3] Tadayoshi Kohdo, Andre Broido and K. C. Claffy, *IEEE Transactions on Dependable and Secure Computing*, (2), April–June 2005.

# Chapter 11

## A CLOSER LOOK AT BIOMETRICS

### FINGERPRINT SCANNERS

Fingerprint scanners are the most widely used form of personal biometric today, due largely to their small size and ease of use. A person simply places his finger on the reader, and he is either granted or denied access. In this section, we will examine the operation of the fingerprint scanner at the device and analysis levels so that technology selection and implementation decisions can be made with better awareness of possible limitations.

At the very beginning, the reader needs to be cautioned that the degree to which a person's fingerprint templates (the recorded characteristics of the finger) are protected while being stored by the operating system may create an easier attack point than trying to break the system by creating a fake fingerprint. These biometric fingerprint scanners should be used with careful attention paid to encryption and protection of the user fingerprint templates. Failure to do so will directly affect the strength of protection offered by the system.

With this caveat in mind, we will examine the four broad classes of fingerprint scanners. The most common class is the optical fingerprint scanner. A second type of reader is the ultrasonic fingerprint scanner; it employs ultrasound to capture the fingerprint. A third class of device is the capacitance fingerprint scanner. And a fourth employs an E-field technology to read the fingerprint. All of these approaches are described in this chapter.

**Optical Fingerprint Scanners**

A fingerprint scanner must begin its process by capturing the detailed microstructure of a person's flesh-toned skin (Figure 11.1). The flesh-toned finger must be illuminated with light striking the finger at a controlled angle, and the light should have spectral properties that will preserve the friction ridges present on the fingertip.

Solid-state optical detectors respond well to red wavelengths, and light-emitting diodes (LEDs) emit red light. Both devices are common, inexpensive, and very compact, so they lend themselves nicely to integration in a fingerprint scanner. Moreover, the combination works well in providing a crisp, black-and-white fingerprint image (Figure 11.2) that can be more easily analyzed than if the captured image were in color.

Note: the two images shown in Figures 11.1 and 11.2 are for illustrative purposes only and are not the same fingerprint.

Optical fingerprint scanners employ fundamental principles of reflection and scattering at air/glass interfaces. In the basic optical configuration used in a fingerprint scanner (shown in Figure 11.3), a finger is placed on a transparent optical surface (usually glass). Ridges in the fingerprint structures make contact with the glass, whereas the valleys between the ridges present air pockets to the glass interface.

Due to the nature of optical reflection at the interface between glass and air, light striking the glass obliquely (indicated by $A_{inc}$) will be strongly reflected when it encounters the glass/air interface (shown by $A_{ref}$). Virtually all of the reflected light will be collected by the lens and the detector, registering that area as a "bright" region. In contrast, if the oblique light encounters an interface between the glass and the ridge of a finger (shown by $B_{inc}$), the light is either absorbed by the ridge of the finger or scattered in many directions ($B_{ref}$). Very little of the reflected light is collected by the lens and the detector, thereby registering the ridge area of the fingerprint as a "dark" region. Much like a conventional fingerprint that is captured by using ink, as shown in Figure 11.2, the fingerprint obtained by an optical scanner registers dark ridges and bright voids.

**Figure 11.1**  A flesh-toned fingerprint.

**Figure 11.2**  A captured black-and-white fingerprint scan.

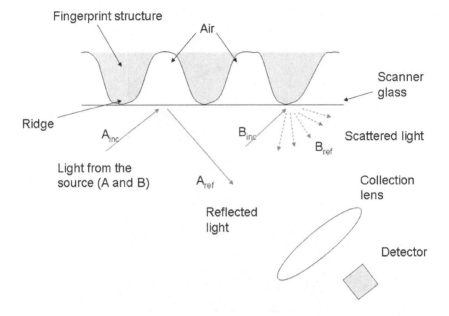

**Figure 11.3** An optical fingerprint scanner.

Within this class, there are two design approaches: a scanner with a narrow line (an imaging array) across which the finger is swiped (Figure 11.3), and a flat scanner device that captures the full fingerprint image without requiring the swiping motion by the user (Figure 11.4).

In order to capture a fingerprint using the swipe type of scanner, the user must brush his finger (generally in a downward motion) across the linear area that comprises the illumination and detection electronics.

Unlike the swipe type of fingerprint scanner pictured in Figure 11.4, the full-image optical scanner (Figure 11.5) presents a full fixed area onto which the user places his finger. Some devices add pressure sensors to detect the presence of the finger, and the image of the fingerprint is captured. It is apparent from the picture above that the demands placed on the full-image scanner by the optical path of an oblique illumination and capture system cause such optical scanners to be somewhat thick. This size can be an issue for integration into smaller devices such as flash thumb drives and laptops.

**Figure 11.4** A two-dimensional fingerprint scanner requiring a swipe.

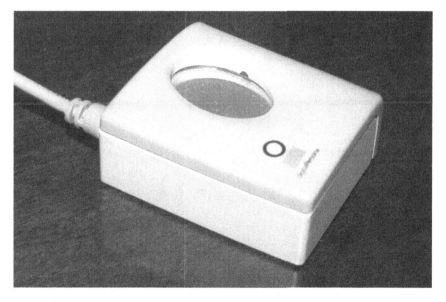

**Figure 11.5** A full-image optical fingerprint scanner.

Optical fingerprint scanners are all sensitive to dirt, oils, and injuries that might be present on the subject's finger. This sensitivity, combined with concerns that optical fingerprint scanners might be easily defeated using silicone "gummy" fingers, has created the demand for alternate fingerprint-scanner technologies.

### Ultrasonic Fingerprint Scanners

An alternate to the optical fingerprint scanner is the ultrasonic fingerprint scanner. This technology takes advantage of a difference in the reflectivity (impedance) between a fingerprint ridge and the air-filled valley. Using an array of sensors and an ultrasonic source, a device can be built that has a spatial resolution of 500 dots per inch or more (by using sensors in the gigahertz range) after processing the reflected signal. This technology can detect the minute features necessary for fingerprint recognition and yet be insensitive to those factors that can affect optical scanners. Moreover, these devices can be made very small, since they do not use the long path that is used in optical scanners.

### Capacitance Fingerprint Scanners

Fingerprint scanners that employ capacitance were developed in the early 1990s. In this device, a silicon-array sensor acts as one plate of a capacitor, and the finger acts as the other.

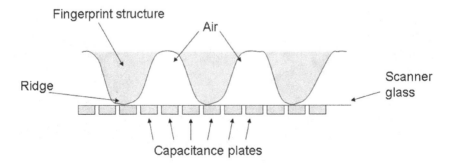

**Figure 11.6**  A capacitance fingerprint scanner.

By using individual sensor plates with a high spatial density (more than 200 per cm, or 500 dpi), it is possible to obtain a gray-scale image of the fingerprint. Both DC and AC capacitance technologies have been implemented, and each sensor element measures the capacitance of the fingerprint element that is directly above the sensor. Since capacitance from neighboring portions of the finger is inevitably part of a single sensor's total measurement, the raw data must be processed to separate this "crosstalk" element of the detector to produce the final image of the fingerprint.

The technology has several advantages over optical fingerprint scanners. First, the capacitance measurement requires a three-dimensional fingerprint rather than a two dimensional image of a fingerprint. This makes faking a fingerprint harder, since a fake must be three-dimensional in order to pass the capacitive sensors. Second, since the detector array is an array of small plates, the entire device can be very compact, certainly much smaller than an optical fingerprint scanner.

A third advantage is that the capacitive sensor can be fabricated very inexpensively, since most components can be made in a semiconductor fabrication process, unlike an optical scanner, which requires an assembly and alignment of several very different elements.

**E-Field Fingerprint Scanners**

Another technology applied to fingerprint capture is called the electric-field or E-field fingerprint scanner. In this device, a signal generator on the reader chip generates an RF signal between the finger and the semiconductor surface. There is a conductive ring layer on the surface that contacts the finger. The RF signal then creates an electric field that mirrors the precise features of the fingerprint. Sensors on the semiconductor chip then capture and process this electric field to produce a captured reproduction of the fingerprint features.

A unique advantage of this technology over the optical and capacitive approaches is that it is not only impervious to dirt, but it is also able to recognize the finger's fingerprint structure even if some accident has destroyed or altered the features on the top surface of the skin.

**THE BASICS OF FINGERPRINT ANALYSIS**

Fingerprint-analysis algorithms used by scanner systems are designed to capture and recognize the same basic features that have been employed by fingerprint-analysis experts for decades. At its core, fingerprint analysis seeks to identify specific minute features (minutiae) within the fingerprint structure and compare them to others in a database. Digital fingerprint scanners can also add other information, such as specific distances between minutiae and the direction of whorls in the fingerprint structure, to further increase the uniqueness of the measurement and thereby decrease FAR and FRR numbers.

In both the classic "ink" type of fingerprint recording and in the digital capture of a fingerprint using one of the technologies listed above, the fingerprint friction ridge, the raised portion that contacts the glass surface of the scanner, is recorded as black, and the fingerprint valley, which is filled with air, is recorded as white. Keeping these in mind, fingerprint experts have developed a list of minutiae that can be found in most fingerprints. The primary minutiae that are employed in fingerprint characterization include:

- *Ridge ending:* a ridge that ends abruptly
- *Bifurcation:* a single ridge that divides into two ridges
- *Lake or enclosure:* a single ridge that bifurcates and reunites shortly afterwards to continue as a single ridge
- *Short ridge (also called island or independent ridge):* a ridge that commences, travels a short distance, and then ends
- *Dot:* a short ridge whose width and length are about equal
- *Spur:* a bifurcation with a short ridge branching off a longer ridge
- *Crossover:* a short ridge that runs between two parallel ridges

In Figure 11.7, we reproduce the fingerprint previously shown in Figure 11.2 at a larger scale and indicate the presence of some of the minutiae listed above.

As explained in previous chapters, fingerprint science is based on two fundamental premises:

- Permanence: more than 100 years of accumulated data have shown that fingerprints do not change during a person's lifetime.
- Uniqueness: no two people have the same fingerprint.

The second premise is very difficult to prove—in fact, the best one could hope to show is that "no identical fingerprints on different people have been found to date." However, mathematical models of the possible ways in which fingerprints can appear suggest that at most only a small number of people have the same fingerprint at any time in a global popu-

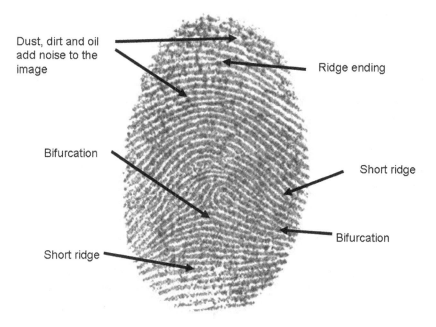

**Figure 11.7**  Minutiae in a sample fingerprint.

lation of 6 billion people. In a paper by Pankanti et al.[1], the authors developed a model of the likelihood of finding a match using fingerprint minutiae. One of their conclusions is that if a fingerprint has 36 minutiae that can be identified, the probability that 12 of those will match an arbitrarily chosen fingerprint from a different person is $6 \times 10^{-8}$. Using the current global population of 6.6 billion people ($6.6 \times 10^9$), there are likely to be 396 matches. Since each person has 10 fingers, this means that at any given moment there are 39 other people in the world who have a fingerprint that will match that of someone being measured. However, the probability that two such people would be involved in a single incident is assumed to be vanishingly small, so the usefulness of the fingerprint as a unique biometric remains intact.

Administrators must be mindful of the realities of the FAR and FRR numbers and their (negative) impact on user verification and overall system security.

## IRIS SCANS

As explained in Chapter 10, iris scanners capture the minute patterns in the iris, the colored region between the pupil and the sclera, and compare these patterns to previously stored iris scans. Iris scans have the advantage that eyeglasses and contact lenses need not be removed for the system to operate properly. A typical iris is shown in Figure 11.8.

The first step in the process is the isolated capture of the iris, without the sclera, pupil, and any light reflections that might be present. This is usually accomplished by smoothing (averaging) the picture so that the disk of the pupil can be more easily identified by software. Figure 11.9 shows a smoothed iris capture.

Next, software locates the best fit circle that just inscribes the pupil (Figure 11.10) and the best circle that captures the outer edge of the iris (Figure 11.11).

The two circles are applied to the unsmoothed image of the eye so that the best-quality capture of the iris is used. Then the annulus between the two circles that contains the iris is converted to a flat rectangle, as shown in Figure 11.12.

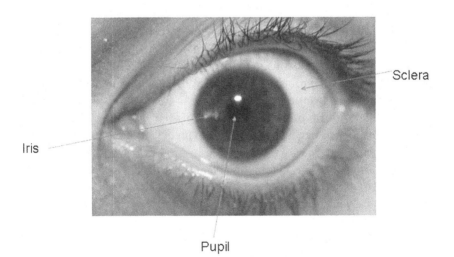

**Figure 11.8** Structure of the eye.

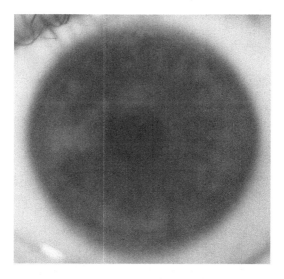

**Figure 11.9**  A smoothed iris capture.

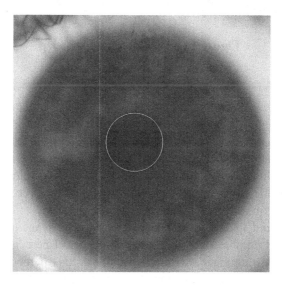

**Figure 11.10**  A circle capturing the edge of the pupil.

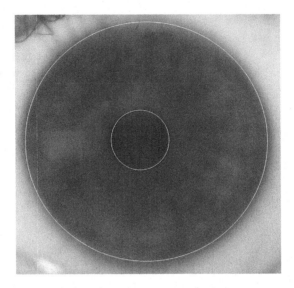

**Figure 11.11** A circle capturing the outer edge of the iris and pupil.

**Figure 11.12** Rectangular iris map.

The rectangular map is not just a conversion of the iris information from radial to rectangular coordinates but also includes the conversion of the iris information to gray scale and a breakdown of the phase information (where along the iris the structure exists) into wavelets. This map is stored as the iris scan of a person and is used to either verify or identify a user at a later time.

The FAR and FRR numbers measured for iris scans are quite good. Reported FRR numbers are often in the range of 0.1 percent (0.001 or 1 in 1000), and FAR numbers are much lower, at 0.0001 percent (0.000001 or 1 in 10,000). Both rates are strikingly better than the rates found with various fingerprint readers, but the usability of an iris scan is not as convenient as that of a fingerprint reader. An administrator and his organization will need to decide on the tradeoff between security and usability when considering iris scans.

There are several important hardware considerations that must be considered in the development and implementation of iris scans. In order to allow the interoperability of various iris-scan systems around the world, a set of standards must be developed that specifies the functional requirements of each of the system elements. This will guarantee that an iris scan obtained using one system will produce the same results with another system. Otherwise, the impressive FRR number cited by manufacturers as measured using just one system will degrade rapidly as a variety of different systems are used. Moreover, variations from one device to the next, even from the same manufacturer, can quickly degrade the FRR numbers. Variability in the image capture and analysis process must be minimized.

## Lens

The lens that images the iris onto the detector is probably the most critical component of an iris-scan system. It must produce an image of the highest possible fidelity without adding its own effects. The lens in an iris-scan system typically must be optimized for operation in the near infrared (long wavelengths between 700 and 1000 nanometers), where the contrast of the iris features is highest. The lens surfaces should have antireflection coatings to maximize throughput and minimize reflections and ghost images. Small pixel size in the detector places demands on the resolution of the lens, which is related to the manufacturing quality of the lens surfaces. Undesirable effects such as diffraction and aberration can affect the image sharpness.

Diffraction is a fundamental result of the fact that a lens will have a finite size. As a result, light from a point source, passing through the lens, produces an alternating pattern of light and dark concentric rings that are referred to as an *airy disk*. The size of the innermost disk is used in calculating the diffraction limit of the lens. The diffraction limit tells a designer the smallest feature that the lens can resolve (also called the *resolution limit*).

The depth of field of the lens must be selected to match the expected operating variations in the imaging step of an iris-scan system. Narrow depth of field can produce out-of-focus conditions more easily than wide designs, but there is a tradeoff between depth of field and resolution that must be considered. Wider depths of field can be achieved with smaller-diameter lenses, but smaller-diameter lenses have resolution limits that get progressively larger with decreasing diameter (that is, the smallest resolvable feature increases with decreasing lens diameter).

Lens aberrations degrade the image by distorting it in various ways. Lenses can introduce different aberrations, including spherical, coma, chromatic, pincushion, astigmatism, and curvature, to name a few. The interested reader should consult any of a number of reference books in optics for more details.

### Detector

The detector must work in close concert with the lens to capture the best possible image of the iris. It should be optimized to operate in the infrared range and should have a resolution compatible with the lens diffraction limit. Ideally it should have no dead (dark) or hot (bright) pixels that would add nonexistent features to the iris image. Its supporting digitizing electronics should provide an acceptable noise figure for the system so that high-integrity images are captured at a variety of operating conditions.

## ILLUMINATION

The illumination system of an iris scanner needs to be bright enough to present high-contrast images through the lens system to the detector yet not be so bright that it damages the eye or irritates the user. Higher light levels allow shorter exposure times, which can be an advantage when movement of the eye during capture is a concern.

### Detector Enclosure

The iris-scanner system (lens, illuminator, and detector) must be packaged in an enclosure, or "camera," that provides stability of the eye during capture, ease of use, user comfort, and minimal contamination of the optics by stray external light.

### Human Interface

In addition to considerations of user comfort and ease of use, the design of the iris scanner must also anticipate and correct for (or be insensitive to) eye, head, and body movement during the image capture. Head and body movements can be largely eliminated by use of a head rest. High-intensity, short-duration light flashes to capture the iris image provide a good tradeoff between minimal movement, good signal to noise, and safety for the user's retina.

The eye naturally scans its environment continuously, performing what are referred to as *saccadic movements* that occur on timescales of a millisecond or so. Such rapid eye movements cannot be stopped and must be considered in setting the design point for an iris scanner.

### Algorithm

The processing algorithm that converts the iris image to the rectangular wavelet map must do so regardless of size, position, and orientation of the subject's eye. Moreover, it must conform to a standard in the presentation of the final iris map, since this is likely to be used by various organizations worldwide to verify a user's identity. Much of the research in the field of iris scans focuses on creating robust algorithms that can handle widely varying conditions and yet produce a stable output that yields a highly reproducible and dependable iris scan.

### RETINAL SCANS

In the 1930s, Simon and Goldstein[2] published a paper in which they reported that the pattern of minute blood vessels in the retina of the eye is unique and could be used as the basis for identifying a person. The eye is protected from the external environment much as the brain is and, as a critical sensory organ, is also protected carefully against injury throughout a person's lifetime. In a subsequent study performed by Dr. Paul Tower[3] in 1955, it was shown that these retinal blood vessels unique, even in the specific case of identical twins, where such a difference is least likely to occur. In fact, Tower showed that, of all the factors that he compared between identical twins, these retinal blood vessels showed the least similarity. See Figure 11.13 for an example of a retinal image.

In the late 1970s, different implementations of retinal scanners appeared on the market. These devices suffered from the need for an expert operator to assure critical alignment of very demanding optics, the need for a bright light due to low detector sensitivity, and high cost. Today, retinal scanners on the market offer smaller size, dramatically reduced light levels, and more forgiving optics (thereby allowing use by a trained technician rather than an expert). Unlike iris scanners, retinal scanners require that the optical path be as undisturbed as possible. This means that contact lenses or eyeglasses must be removed for the scan to work properly.

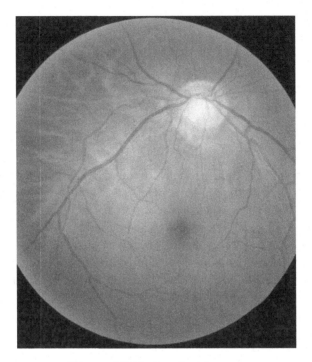

**Figure 11.13**  A retinal image.

Retinal scanners, like iris scanners, have a lens, an illumination source, a detector, an enclosure, a human interface, and processing algorithms. (They also require a scanner, which is not present on an iris scan.) Many of the technical requirements placed on these elements match those previously presented in the section on iris scans above and will not be repeated here. However, retinal scanners present their own specific demands on the technology elements, and these are discussed below.

**Illumination**

Unlike an iris scan, the illumination used in a retinal scanner must pass through the lens of the eye (through the pupil), illuminate the retina, and then reflect back through the pupil for reimaging onto the detector. This requires much more light than is used in an iris scan, so much so that infrared LEDs must be of a higher intensity than is used in an iris scanner. An incandescent source can also be used and in fact improves the signal-to-noise ratio of the captured image, but this adds size, heat, and bulb-lifetime issues to the device. There is work being done on identifying an acceptable laser source, although the perceived safety concerns will likely increase.

### Detector

The demands on the illumination system can be mitigated somewhat by using more sensitive detectors, but today's IR-sensitive solid-state cameras operate at nearly the noise limit of sensitivity.

### Scanner

Like an iris scan, the retinal scan defines an annular region in the retina that will be used to determine the user's retinal signature. The retina is much larger than an iris, so a mechanical scan must be performed after alignment in order to capture the entire annulus (see Figure 11.14). The

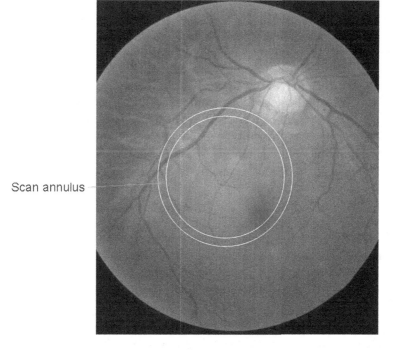

Scan annulus

**Figure 11.14**  The Retinal Scan Annulus.

scanning process converts the annulus into a time stream (analogous to the rectangular iris map) that is then converted using a fast-fourier-transform (FFT) process to a signature. The retinal scan system measures about 400 points in the blood-vessel patterns within the retinal image. Each data point is digitized to up to 4096 bits (12 bits). This signature is later used for verification or recognition.

### Enclosure

The more open the user's pupil is during the scan, the less light will be needed to get a good image. The ability of the enclosure to isolate the eye against stray light goes a long way towards allowing a dark-adapted eye to present an open pupil to the retinal scanner.

### User Interface

There are a variety of user constraints that make the technology less than ideal for use in general applications. First, the user must remove any eyeglasses that he might be wearing. Otherwise, reflections from the lens may disturb the actual signal, and distortion and refraction may make repeatability from session to session difficult, resulting in false rejections. Second, the eye must be placed close to the device (typically within 1/2 inch), and the user must focus on a certain point for several seconds without blinking. Finally, the scan requires several seconds for capture, during which time the head and eye must remain still. Remaining processing can add another 10 seconds, depending on the algorithm, database size, etc. Most general users find the technology (unjustifiably) threatening, since the eye is placed in close proximity to the imaging optics and must be held open for the duration of the capture. This is only a perceived risk to the eye but is certainly deemed by most users to be somewhat uncomfortable.

### Performance

There is no known way to replicate the complete eye lens/pupil/retina system. Moreover, the retina from a dead person would deteriorate too rapidly to be useful. As a result, most retinal scan systems today do not take any extra precautions to assure that the retina being scanned comes from a live person.

A 1991 study performed at Sandia National Laboratory by Holmes et al.[4] reported no false accepts in more than one million possible matches in the test database and an FRR of 1 percent. These numbers place the reti-nal-scan technology in a strong position for environments that demand high security. Cost and user comfort remain issues that inhibit broader adoption of the technology, but its low measured FRR and FAR numbers make it popular for use in high-security environments (such as nuclear-power plants).

## REFERENCES

[1] Pankanti, S., Prabhakar, S., and Jain, A., "On the individuality of fingerprints," *IEEE Trans. Pattern Anal. Machine Intell.*, 24 8, 2002, pp. 1010–1025.

[2] C. Simon and I. Goldstein, "A New Scientific Method of Identification," *New York State Journal of Medicine*, Vol. 35, No. 18, September, 1935, pp. 901–906.

[3] P. Tower, "The fundus Oculi in monozygotic twins: Report of six pairs of iden-tical twins," *Archives of Ophthalmology*, Vol. 54, 1955, pp. 225–239.

[4] J.P. Holmes, L. J. Wright and R. L. Maxwell, *A Performance Evaluation of Biometric Identification Devices*, Technical Report SAND91-0276, UC-906, Sandia National Laboratories, Albuquerque, NM 87185 and Livermore, CA 94550 for the United States Department of Energy under Contract DEAC04-76DP00789, 1991.

# Chapter 12

## TOKENS: SOMETHING YOU HAVE

### OVERVIEW

Classic physical security practices often involve the use of two authentication factors: something you know and something you have. Examples of the first are a username, password, PIN number, or pass phrase. Examples of the second might include a door key and a photo ID. In order to gain access to a building or a room, you must have something that grants you that access.

In the computer-security world, "something you have" (a token) needs to be able to interact with software gatekeepers. Examples of such tokens will be examined in more detail in this chapter.

Of course, all tokens used in a security system have the same usability issue—if left behind (at the office, at home, or in a hotel room, to name some examples), the person will be unable to authenticate himself using the technology. This sometimes causes system administrators to turn away from such required tokens, using software-only approaches instead. This decision usually opens an organization up to the attack vectors common in software-only security systems and is not recommended.

## RADIO-FREQUENCY IDS

Radio-frequency IDs (RFIDs) usually consist of a small set of passive electronics and an antenna packaged together to form a transponder within a flat, credit-card-sized object. The antenna and electronics are designed to respond only to a very narrow range of radio frequencies, and the electronics further restrict the signals to those that have features (bits) that have been preprogrammed into the card. Unlike infrared remote controls, RFIDs do not require line-of-sight contact with the transmitter—radio waves travel around and/or through various types of common obstructions.

The specific frequency used by an RFID system will be determined to some extent by the range requirements of the application. Physical access cards have ranges of less than 1 foot and operate at frequencies of 125–134 kHz. Product-identification applications (including inventory control) use RFIDs that operate at 13.5 MHz and have ranges on the order of 3 feet or more. Longer-range RFIDs operate at frequencies from 1 to 6 GHz. There are two types of RFIDs: active and passive.

### Passive RFID

When a passive RFID card receives a signal (a query) within the right frequency range and with the right sequence of bits, it uses the incoming RF waves to charge a capacitor on the card. The capacitor acts as a short-term battery, and it energizes a transmitting portion of the card's electronics. The transmitting electronics send out a "response," a different sequence of bits, and this response is then received by the transmitter that sent the original RF query. Typical capacity for an RFID is 128 bytes. The response might, for example, include the name and access privileges of the person carrying the card. Software running the query transmitter uses this new information to examine a database of authorized users, and it then acts upon the result. For example, a recognized user might be granted access to a locked room, or a gate to a parking garage might open. Of course, this technology is not limited to physical uses. RFIDs can be used to grant the holder access to a PC by unlocking the desktop when the user places his RFID near a query station. RFIDs can also be used in conjunction with other authentication mechanisms, such as the successful entry of a password or PIN number to complement the presence of the RFID.

Passive RFIDs only become active within range of a querying station that is transmitting the correct binary sequence. The usable range is typically 10–15 feet, although some are much shorter. Their cost is about 20 cents each, placing them within range of the cost of barcodes (which are about a penny each).

Passive RFID technology is often used in inventory control. These low-cost, very thin devices can be used to hold product-number information. When a querying transmitter activates the unit, it responds with its product ID, which can then be added to a running total as the inventory manager walks through a warehouse. Collision detection and one-way inventory addition assure that the software will only tally a unit once and will keep multiple transponder responses separate while each is handled individually.

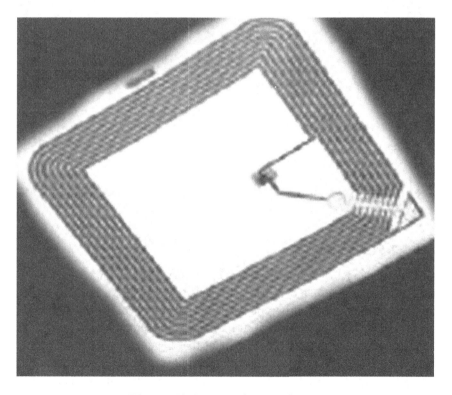

**Figure 12.1** A passive RFID tag.

**Figure 12.2** A passive RFID in a card.

## Active RFIDs

Unlike passive RFIDs, an active RFID contains a battery and does not use the RF wave to charge a capacitor. It is able to broadcast as soon as it recognizes a valid query. This type of RFID is used on highways for automated toll collection. The range of these transponders is larger, up to 300 feet. Data capacity is still 128 bytes, but that is generally sufficient for a unique transmission of requested information. Active RFIDs can also be used in conjunction with other authentication mechanisms, such as the entry of a PIN number under certain conditions.

## RFID Attack Vectors

A common secure implementation of RFID technology facilitates transactions using an RFID token. In this application, a 24-bit (three-character) serial number is sent to a query station. The station then uses the serial number to access a user database to extract the expected signature. It then "asks" the RFID to send its 40-bit (five-character) signature, which is then compared to that in the database. If they match, a purchase is then authorized.

The small size of the factors in the challenge-response process is clearly an opening for an attack. The cryptography used to create the five-character signature has been determined to be rather weak, but even so, a brute force attack to determine the signature could be easily accomplished by a dedicated processor in a matter of a couple of hours. Moreover, if the signature is somehow derived from the serial number, then the attack space is even smaller. Successful attacks of this sort have been documented by various research groups, but the details have been suppressed to avoid propagation of the technique, thereby creating fraud and theft. The researchers were able to obtain the initial serial numbers by electronic eavesdropping, and then brute-force attack methods were applied to the results until they broke the system.

### RF Sniffing

Passive Rfids (and most active Rfids as well) are usually static in order to minimize cost and maximize their use in the commercial sector. As a result, the data transmitted by the device in response to the query from the RF broadcasting station usually does not change. If an attacker can obtain a valid RFID from an unsuspecting victim (or worse, from an insider), an inexpensive electronic antenna placed in the vicinity of the RFID during the access process should be able to capture the data for a later replay attack. Low-cost RFID cards do not include on-board encryption and cost about 25 cents; those with encryption technology cost about $5. Even building-access systems typically do not employ the more expensive encryption-protected RFID technology but rather use the lower-cost static form.

RFID tags are used to protect an increasingly diverse set of products. They can be found in gasoline-pump purchases, access to automobiles as the owner approaches, building and parking-lot access, and neighborhood gated communities, in addition to their widespread use for inventory control and theft detection. As the item being protected increases in value, better methods to defeat or steal the RFID access will be developed.

Estimates vary, but the current worldwide market size for RFID technology in 2007 has been reported to be anywhere from $1 billion to $3 billion, with significant growth in the coming years.

Attacks on nonencrypted RFIDs can often be accomplished with very small, inexpensive hardware and software. A commercially available RFID reader/writer can be purchased and used in conjunction with software to easily examine the contents of an RFID and overwrite the contents with new information if the storage section of the RFID has not been write-protected. But write protection does not facilitate the use of the technology in situations where the protected items are continually being removed and later returned (as in a library environment, for example). Errors in implementation procedures can further compromise the security of the system.

Copy-and-paste attacks can also be used to compromise RFID protection in commercial sales environments. Using hardware and software similar to that described above, an attacker can "copy" RFID tag information from a low-cost baseball, for example, and "paste" the information into the RFID tag of an expensive baseball. If the watchful eye of a checkout clerk is not involved, more complex copy/paste attacks can be performed, such as copying a hotel room key's RFID tag into that of a library book. In that case, the library book can be used to open the hotel room.

The use of a tested encryption technology is important in installations that employ the cryptographic protection feature. There have been reports of untested RFID encryption algorithms being broken by sophisticated attackers. It should be noted that cryptographic RFIDs can offer significant protection even if the encryption is not tested. Unlike the techniques described above, even untested encryption algorithms require advanced cryptographic skills to defeat the system.

RFIDs have been implemented in multifactor authentication systems to protect against copying the tag's contents. In new US passports, for example, RFID chips within the passport require that the passport be physically open before the transponder will respond to queries. This protects against casual copying while the passport is closed within someone's purse or pocket. Moreover, much like the CID number on a credit card, the passports also include a password that is printed in machine-readable code (a bar code) that must also be present before the RFID will be recognized.

One of the more controversial uses of RFID technology is its use as a personal implant. In principle, an implanted RFID would contain an ID number that would be linked to a person's medical records, his room or building access, his car, and more. Because it is implanted, it cannot be lost or stolen. The implants are small, about the size of a long grain of rice.

Of most concern is the security of the existing technology, its protection against rewriting attacks and copying, personal privacy, and the technology's extendibility to stronger cryptography as techniques move forward. Currently implant RFIDs use a frequency very similar to those used by regular passive RFIDs, so they can be read by existing RFID readers. The implants contain a 16-digit number, which is equivalent to 128 bits. Unlike the use of this 128-bit number as a key in cryptography that must be guessed, the 128-bit ID number in the implant merely needs to be read. The use of a reader of appropriate sensitivity in the vicinity of the person's arm can reveal the ID number without the target's knowledge. Once captured, the ID number can be "pasted" into a blank RFID, and the person's privileges have been stolen. The small size of the implant precludes the use of encryption in the unit (at least using today's technologies), so the copy/paste attack can be executed easily. The only remedy would be the use of the technology in conjunction with something else (additional authentication factors such as a password), but the convenience of the technology begins to fade as more cumbersome factors are added.

Rfids are a modest first level of defense in a security system, but until the attack issues have been addressed, the technology should be viewed with caution.


## SMART CARDS

Smart cards are generally (but not always) credit-card size and include a thin chip that has an array of contacts on the outside surface. The chip typically includes a secure coprocessor, cryptographic algorithms, and protected storage. There are a limited set of commands that can be communicated across the contact interface, and these include a mixture of encrypted and plain-text commands. Secure functions can only be accessed through the encrypted commands. Exceptions to the card format include the use of the smart-card chip in an RF-connected token that operates when in proximity to an approved reader, but the core technology remains the same.

Smart cards are another form of token ("something you have") that users can carry and present on demand. The smart card is placed into a smart-card reader. An example of a smart card and a reader are shown in Figure 12.3. The contacts can be seen on the right end of the smart card closest to the reader.

For contact smart cards, the gold contacts connect to properly positioned electrical "fingers" within the smart-card reader when the card is

**Figure 12.3** A smart card and reader.

inserted fully into it, and commands can then be issued to the reader by the application. There are also contactless smart cards that use RF to communicate over a short range to a reader. Although much more popular in Europe, bank credit and debit cards in the US are increasingly being delivered to customers with smart-card chips embedded in them as an additional source of secure information to complement the magnetic stripe. Unlike magnetic stripes, the smart-card chip contains much more memory, enabling the use of the technology for storage of critical personal or financial information. The US Department of Defense uses a smart card as the basis for its common-access card (CAC) system.

Smart cards can be used to authenticate a user, present healthcare information to a hospital or other provider, or run specific applications, such as enabling a cable TV box for premium service delivery. Not only must the user have the smart card in his possession, but he must also be able to enter his name and/or password/PIN number in order to gain access to protected functions or spaces. Due to their thin size, they are easily carried in a purse or wallet without much resistance from users.

Since the smart card has encryption and a coprocessor on the chip, there is no security concern about hackers eavesdropping on bus channels to pick up information—the only information that is presented by the user is his name and pass phrase, and without possession of the original smart card, a hacker has no hope of defeating the protected system.

When a smart card is placed into a smart-card reader, the coprocessor on the card generates a random number, which it then passes to the application that is controlling the reader. The application then encrypts the random number with a key that has been shared with the smart card and returns the encrypted random number to the smart card. The coprocessor on the smart card duplicates the process, using its known encryption algorithm and its copy of the shared key to encrypt the random number. The encrypted random number generated by the reader is compared to the one generated by the smart card's coprocessor; if they match, a secure communication can begin. The two parties can then exchange a session key, and both can verify the authenticity of any subsequent communication during the session by using the same process to encrypt a hash summary of the data packet. This allows for detection of false data in the pathway. All further communications between the card and the reader are encrypted, thereby thwarting hackers. Smart cards can use a variety of encryption algorithms, but the most common are DES, 3DES, and RSA's public key cryptography.

**Smart-Card Attack Vectors**

Smart cards store their data in an electrically erasable programmable read-only memory (EEPROM). As its name implies, an EEPROM can be erased when subjected to certain electrical conditions. In a practical sense, this means that the application of an unusual voltage can cause the EEPROM to be erased, thereby possibly removing the security defenses of the card. Studies have also shown that exposure to extreme heat or ultraviolet light can destroy security protection on smart cards. Of course, direct physical attack can also be performed, in which case the attacker can ultimately learn the layout of the smart card's circuitry, thereby possibly enabling him to create a convincing fake or enabling him to defeat a protected card. Of course, more costly and complex attacks using x-rays or focused ion-beam probes have also been reported, although their cost and complexity tend to limit the usefulness of these attacks.

Direct physical attacks can be made progressively more difficult by using smaller and smaller lithographic processes (line widths) to manufacture the smart-card chips.

A technique called differential power analysis (DPA) and a closely related approach called simple power analysis (SPA) have been successfully used to extract encryption keys from smart cards. In these attacks, the smart card is fed an input string, and the demand on the power consumption being used by the smart card is analyzed. It is possible to identify which cryptographic algorithm is being used and when the cryptographic processes are being employed. By using carefully designed queries or monitoring different uses of the card over time, it is possible to identify data-dependent differences in the response of the system. Over many such queries, a progressively better guess of the encryption key can be developed, and ultimately the encryption key being used can be deduced. Some systems have been broken in a matter of seconds using this technique, usually without the card holder's knowledge that an attack has been completed.

The use of the random-number generator within the smart card's chip can be used to introduce unpredictable demands on the power, thereby making the DPA and SPA approaches difficult if not impossible to employ.

Random clock jitter does not protect the actual contents of the smart card but rather makes the DPA and SPA attacks much more difficult to complete. Alternative attacks have since been identified. In a study performed at Cambridge University, Skorobogatov and Anderson[1] demonstrated that information stored within a smart card can be revealed by stripping off the top protective layer of the chip and illuminating it with a brief flash of light. Using light from low-cost sources (a camera flash and a laser pointer), the authors reported that they were able to induce local ionization in the memory cells of the chip, causing bits to flip to the complementary state. The authors reported that they were able to flip any individual bit within an SRAM chip using this technique. This technique can be used to reverse the protection settings on the chip, thereby allowing write functions that were previously prohibited. The authors also demonstrated that altering specific bits can alter the execution path of smart-card code.

The SRAM structure is usually employed for storing keys and other static information and often includes information about the memory map, which is critical to a reverse-engineering attack. This technique allowed both probing and altering of information that was stored in the chip without requiring high-precision micromechanical actuators.

Although the optical-flash attack requires stripping off the top protective layer of the smart-card chip, it still has advantages over more costly focused-ion beam probes and micromechanical actuator techniques. The optical-flash technique does not involve making electrical contact with the metal surface, thereby simplifying the attack. The group also recommended a possible protection against such an attack by altering the circuit design.

## INTERACTIVE TOKENS

The need for usability sometimes works against the need for security. For example, people generally prefer passwords that never change or at most change once a year. They also prefer passwords that are easy to remember (see Chapter 3). These two preferences run counter to good security practices, which ideally would use a password that is used only once and changes each time. A class of hardware token has been developed that bridges this gap. An example of such a token is RSA's SecurID®, shown in Figure 12.4.

**Figure 12.4** RSA's SecurID® hardware token.

This token contains a precision built-in clock, a PRG, and an initial seed that is usually set at the time the token is issued. Each token has a different seed, and the seed for a specific token is stored in a secure database on a server under a profile corresponding to the user and token ID. Once issued, the token generates and displays a random number on its screen and changes the displayed number at a fixed time interval (usually once every 30 or 60 seconds). The set of bars visible in the left portion of the token screen shown in Figure 12.4 is a visible indication of the remaining time before the number changes, thereby reducing the number of partial entries that might otherwise occur if a user does not know how much time remains. The token has several tamper-proof features that prevent reverse engineering or other compromises to the operation of the token.

In use, the user accesses a secure web page and is then challenged to enter his username or user ID and his password. The password consists of a fixed password (constant and set by the user when the token was issued) appended with the number that is displayed on his token at the time of login. Since the server has a real time clock and "knows" the user's password, seed, and PRG algorithm, it is able to calculate the number that is being displayed on the specific user's token at the time of login. It can therefore verify that the username, password, and appended displayed number match what is expected at the time of login. The displayed number changes once every 30 or 60 seconds, so a password combination (fixed password plus appended displayed number) is used only once. This satisfies the usability need for a fixed password and yet also satisfies the need for a password that is used only once and changes each time. Some implementations include the option for entering a "duress code," a fixed number that tells the server that the user has been forced to enter his PIN number. This usually allows authentication to proceed so that the attacker is not alerted to the fact that an unusual PIN has been entered. The system administrator is then alerted that a breach is underway.

### Synchronization

Tokens that employ the timer and challenge/response process described above may fall out of temporal synchronization with the server from time to time. Since the server and the token would not be calculating the same displayed number at the same time, this could prevent a legitimate user from authenticating himself to the server for access. There is a method in place for resynchronizing the token with the main server to correct this situation.

## Token Attack Vectors

### Seed Attacks

The seed that initializes the token's PRG is often sent to the user as an ASC file. If the file is stored on the computer in an unprotected area, a sophisticated attacker may succeed in obtaining the file. With this, the attacker is able to reproduce the entire past, present, and future history of random numbers that will be displayed by the token. (See the section on PRGs in Chapter 3.) Tools can be downloaded that perform this function using the ASC file. Care must be taken to store the file on offline storage separate from the token as soon as the token has been initialized.

With the knowledge of the number that is displayed by a target token at any time, the only remaining task for the attacker is to determine the fixed password that the user employs. Dictionary attacks can be mounted to determine the password, and success can be achieved quickly if the password is very simple. Without knowledge of the random number being displayed, the consequent large attack space for the token will likely render cracking it virtually impossible.

### Man-in-the-Middle Attacks

As explained previously, a man-in-the-middle attack occurs when the attacker inserts himself between the user and the server. In the case of the token, the attacker cannot replace the user's credentials with his credentials, since a copy exists on a remote server. Rather, the attacker must pass the user's credentials on to the server in order to complete the authentication. If he has successfully compromised the communication between the server and the user, he is then fully able to capture the information traveling between the two for the duration of the session and can insert his own information or requests as well.

## REFERENCES

[1] B.S. Kaliski Jr. et al. (eEds.), *CHES 2002, LNCS 2523*, Springer-Verlag, 2003, pp. 2–12, 2003. "Double-Size Bipartite Modular Multiplication," Springer-Verlag Berlin Heidelberg 2003.

# Chapter 13

## LOCATION TECHNOLOGIES

### OVERVIEW

As user and PC mobility increase, location is becoming more important. In some cases, its value is realized in applications that provide the mobile user with location-related information, such as hotels, restaurants, and driving directions. In other cases, location becomes a means for asset tracking. Location can also be used as an access-control parameter in DRM applications (as discussed in Chapter 8), controlled-access information based on location, or location-based information sharing. Other environments foster complete freedom of user movement without regard to location.

### LOCATION'S PLACE IN SECURITY

In applications or user environments where location is immaterial, location technologies are not likely to be employed as part of the user security architecture. However, even in those environments, there is a need to provide the mobile user with some assurance that the remote server that he is accessing is indeed a valid server and that he has not been redirected to a carefully constructed duplicate that is using his information for other purposes. This type of server spoofing is a common element of the social-engineering attack called phishing, which has been described previously in this book. Knowledge (and validation) of the physical location of the valid server could provide protection to the mobile user, even if the user's location is immaterial to the specific information-sharing architecture that he is using.

In order for location information to play a valuable role in security, it must not be easily spoofed. The ability of an attacker to guess a person's location information or to capture that location information for later replay attacks is an example of weak location technologies. Moreover, the ability of an attacker to duplicate location information through artificial means can also create a weakness in the implementation of location in security architectures.

Location's role in the security paradigm lies somewhere between "something you have" and "something you know." The location of a user or a PC is established through the presentation of the correct location credentials as part of a challenge/response process. The creation of these location credentials becomes the task of the location technology being employed. Specific examples of location technologies and their attack vectors are discussed in subsequent sections of this chapter. Rather than create security architectures in which the location credential is treated as a hybrid of "something you have" and "something you know," it is best to use location as a separate credential, perhaps "where are you now." As discussed below, some implementations employ a historical record of locations as yet another credential, "where have you been."

## GEOLOCATION

To best understand the use of geolocation technologies and possible attack vectors on these implementations, it is helpful to review the principles used in the operation of GPS. GPS employs a constellation of 24 solar-powered high-earth-orbit satellites that complete their orbits every 12 hours. Orbital planes and positions of the satellites have been selected to provide as much global coverage as possible at any given time. In general, 4 to 12 GPS satellites are above the horizon at any point on the earth. The satellites are at an altitude of about 12,000 miles.

Each satellite has a built-in high-precision clock that is synchronized with all the other satellites. The satellites emit timing pulses once a second at two different frequencies; one (called L1) operates at 1.2 GHz, and the other (L2) operates at 1.5 GHz. Most GPS receivers (such as those used by hikers) just use L1 timing pulses in order to simplify the receiver electronics and minimize cost and size. Units that employ both frequencies are able to provide advanced ionospheric corrections and obtain higher positioning accuracy. More expensive dual-frequency units are usually used in surveying operations in which higher precision is required.

In considering the use of GPS for geolocation sensing, the most general solution is one in which we seek knowledge of the receiver's location in three dimensions. In doing so, we remove the restriction that the receiver must reside on the surface of the Earth.

Each timing pulse is emitted with a time stamp that indicates when the pulse left satellite 1 (we will call this departure time $t_{departure\ 1}$). By noting the time of arrival ($t_{arrival\ 1}$) at the receiver, it is possible to determine the travel time ($t_{travel\ 1} = t_{arrival\ 1} - t_{departure\ 1}$) from the satellite to the receiver. Since radio waves travel at the speed of light c, the distance from the satellite to the receiver must be $D_1 = c * t_{travel\ 1}$. With this information, we can conclude that the receiver lies somewhere on a sphere of radius $D_1$ centered on the satellite as shown in Figure 13.1.

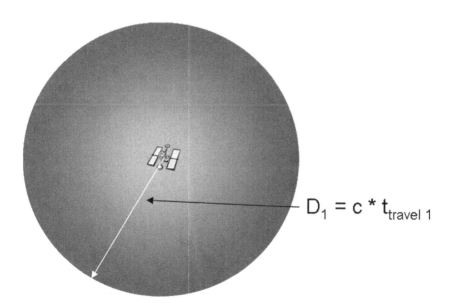

**Figure 13.1**  Geolocation knowledge with one satellite.

In order to better constrain the knowledge of the location of the receiver, the process must be repeated with the timing signals from a second satellite. Using measurements of the travel time from a second satellite and knowing the location of the two satellites in space (obtained from the orbital data that is broadcast periodically by the satellites), a second measurement reveals that the receiver must be somewhere where the two spheres intersect, as shown in Figure 13.2.

The actual geolocation of the receiver must lie somewhere on the ring that describes the intersection of the two spherical surfaces, as shown in Figure 13.2. In order to further refine the knowledge of location, the process for adding a sphere based on timing signals must be repeated for a third satellite. Upon doing so, the possible locations for the receiver are reduced to two points, as shown in Figure 13.3.

For complete knowledge of the receiver's geolocation in three dimensions, the ambiguity between the two possible locations shown in Figure 13.3 can be removed by adding a timing signal from a fourth satellite.

**Key Requirements for Proper Operation of Geolocation**

Geolocation technologies require several elements in order to provide authentic location information:

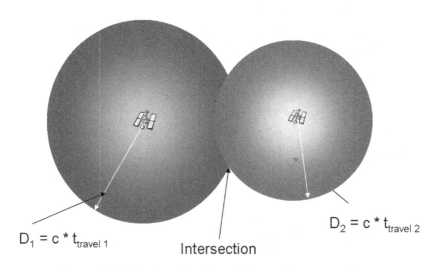

$$D_1 = c * t_{travel\ 1}$$

Intersection

$$D_2 = c * t_{travel\ 2}$$

**Figure 13.2** Geolocation knowledge with two satellites.

- Signal strength: The timing signals used in the geolocation system must be sufficiently strong that they can be detected within large office buildings or in urban settings. GPS receivers often are unable to receive sufficient signal strength to allow operation within buildings. The use of repeaters could be employed, but then the location of the units that are receiving signals from the repeater will report a location that corresponds only to the repeater's location.

- Time: In order to determine a timing pulse's time of arrival so that the travel time can be determined, the receiver must have an accurate knowledge of the current time. This is usually achieved by using the time provided by the satellite as a first approximation. Since the travel time from a GPS satellite is approximately 600 milliseconds, this approximation quickly yields an accurate time as more satellites are recognized by the electronics.

- Orbital information: The direction of all the satellites is required so that the measured travel times ultimately yield a three-dimensional position of the receiver relative to the constellation of satellites (and therefore relative to the earth). Since it is not possible to know in

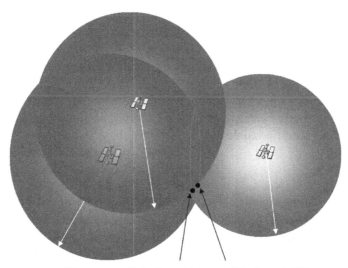

Two possible locations with 3 satellites

**Figure 13.3**  Geolocation knowledge with three satellites.

advance which satellites will be observable by the receiver electronics, it is necessary to retain knowledge of all 24 satellites. This orbital information is available through websites and is also broadcast by all of the satellites continuously, although the validity of the data expires anywhere from 2 hours to 7 days, depending on various conditions.

- Initial location: In principle, if the receiver has no prior guess as to its location, it could be anywhere on the earth and therefore be receiving signals from any of the 24 satellites located nearly anywhere in the sky. By providing the receiver with an initial "guess" as to its probable location, the receiver can reduce the search space to the most likely positions of the satellites that are expected to be visible from that location.

### Assisted GPS

By providing time, complete orbital information, and an initial location "guess," GPS receivers can be "assisted" so that they can obtain a location fix in about a minute or less. GPS receivers built into cellular phones often obtain assist information from the cellular tower to get a lock quickly. Once a fix has been obtained, the unit can maintain a lock on the satellites (provided they have sufficient signal strength, of course) without further assistance from the tower.

## GEOLOCATION ATTACK VECTORS

An attack on a geolocation technology such as GPS would involve the subversion of one or more of the elements listed above that are required for proper operation. These attacks, combined with the architecture of the security system that seeks to employ location as an authentication parameter, create a list of possible attack points for these technologies.

### Jammers

Since GPS timing signals bathe the entire half of the earth that is facing a specific satellite, the signal strength at a small, handheld receiver on the earth is relatively weak. The GPS signal strength measured at the earth's surface is about $1 \times 10^{-16}$ watts. In contrast, a cellular telephone typically receives $2 \times 10^{-1}$ watts, which is two million billion times stronger. By adding lots of noise into the RF spectrum at the two GPS frequencies, it is possible to reduce the SNR sufficiently that a GPS receiver cannot discern any satellite timing signals from the intense noise. These jammers are low-cost devices and could potentially be positioned in the vicinity of targeted GPS units. The only remaining defense against such jamming is the degree to which the software properly handles a situation where no location is reported.

## Attenuation

An alternate method of reducing a receiver's ability to detect satellite signals is to attenuate the signals to the point where they cannot be detected above the electronic noise in the receiver. This is more invasive than the jamming attack, since the best way to accomplish this would be to wrap the receiver in layers of aluminum foil, thereby creating a Faraday cage into which no signals can penetrate. However, if an attacker can get physical possession of a secure location device and wishes to defeat its defenses in the privacy of his own facility, such an attack is not unreasonable. Once again, the software becomes the last line of defense against such an attack. It is important that the software handle the report of "no location available" properly so that no security exposure is created.

## Artificial Constellations

GPS manufacturers and labs that conduct research and development in GPS technologies often employ GPS generators to provide strong artificial geolocation signals within the facility for testing and evaluation purposes. Such GPS generators emit timing signals and orbital data that mimic a true constellation but at a stronger level. Since these units are commercially available, an attacker could easily employ such a unit to broadcast this artificial constellation over a broad area, thereby spoofing any receivers in the area into concluding that their geolocation corresponds to the generator's location. In effect, an attacker could "dial in" any coordinates he desired to help defeat a security system that would be requesting location authentication as part of its challenge-response process.

## Fraudulent Timing Pulses

A more sophisticated (and costly) form of jamming attack involves the broadcast of artificial timing pulses at the two primary GPS frequencies. Unlike jamming, which renders the receiver incapable of extracting timing signals at all from the high noise environment, this approach serves to destroy the unit's ability to maintain a valid determination of travel time.

Without this information, the receiver is unable to determine its geolocation, thereby preventing the unit from submitting valid geolocation credentials as part of an authentication process.

### Corruption of Assist and Initial Location Information

The files used to provide the orbital, time, and initial location information to an assisted GPS device must be protected against attack through judicious use of encryption. Failure to do so creates a possible attack avenue in which such files are replaced with altered files. The impact of such a replacement would be that the unit would search for the wrong satellites in the wrong part of the sky at the wrong time. This would increase the amount of time before such a unit could obtain a fix on the actual satellites, thereby preventing the delivery of location information that might be needed for location-based authentication. Moreover, the data path along which such assist information is provided to the device must also be protected against unauthorized access. Failure to do so allows an attacker a means by which undesirable commands and data can be fed into the GPS chip set, possibly changing communication parameters and altering assist information so that the unit becomes effectively unresponsive.

### Possible Protection Measures

In all cases described above, it is important that the authentication system that is relying upon location as an authentication parameter handle null conditions securely. That is, in the event that a reported location is not available, the authentication software must deny the user access and disconnect him from the system. Alternatively, such a null condition might require that the user enter an additional, separate, and seldom used authentication factor (a second password or biometric) before location-independent access is granted.

Signal strengths of GPS satellites do not typically exceed certain thresholds, nor do they typically experience large excursions in values. Monitoring of these figures could be used to detect the possible presence of an attack. An alert could be used in conjunction with an authentication system to notify the administrator that the data from a specific user appears suspicious, and the user's authentication could be denied or suspended until the matter is investigated.

GPS receivers usually obtain an accurate time from the constellation of satellites. Significant deviations of the GPS time from the system clock might provide a means by which an attack could be detected.

In all cases, designers must be careful to avoid introducing a new attack point by inadvertently handling unusual conditions involving GPS.

## WI-FI HOT-SPOT TRIANGULATION

Wireless access points (commonly referred to as "Wi-Fi") emit radio beacons that include an identifier of the access point. These beacons are received by wireless network cards present in various mobile devices such as laptops and handheld devices. In regular operation, users configure their units to login to selected access points (using passwords if required) to provide access to the Internet.

Multiple Wi-Fi units within an office or building can be used to locate a mobile device by measuring the relative signal strengths as measured by the device. Since signal strength is associated with a specific unit's identifier, it is possible to infer an approximate location of a receiver using this approach. In Figure 13.4, three Wi-Fi hotspots are signified by different numbers (1, 2 and 3). As a reasonable first approximation, the signal strength of the Wi-Fi signal decreases with the inverse fourth power of the distance from the source. The decrease in signal strength with distance is represented pictorially by the decrease in darkness of the image with distance from its numbered Wi-Fi hotspot.

In operation as a location technology, software on a user's mobile device measures the relative strengths of the multiple Wi-Fi hotspots within range and reports those strengths back to a central server that is authenticating the user's location. Using a map of the relative signal strengths for the building, it is possible to get a reasonable fix on the device's location.

In Figure 13.4, the three hotspots (labeled 1, 2 and 3) can be assumed to have circular radiation patterns that follow the inverse fourth law behavior. A user's device located at mobile position A, for example, will measure approximately equal signal strengths from sources 2 and 3, and much weaker signal strength from source 1. A device located at position B will measure slightly stronger signals from source 2, weaker from source 1, and much weaker signal strength from source 3. Finally, a device located at position C will measure the strongest signals from source 1, less but similar strength from source 3, and much weaker signal strength from source 2. Presented in a simple tabular fashion, the three locations might report the following relative signal strengths. The values are shown for illustrative purposes only and do not represent actual measured data.

A lookup table can be used with a map of the relative signal strengths to convert a reported set of signal-strength numbers directly to a location.

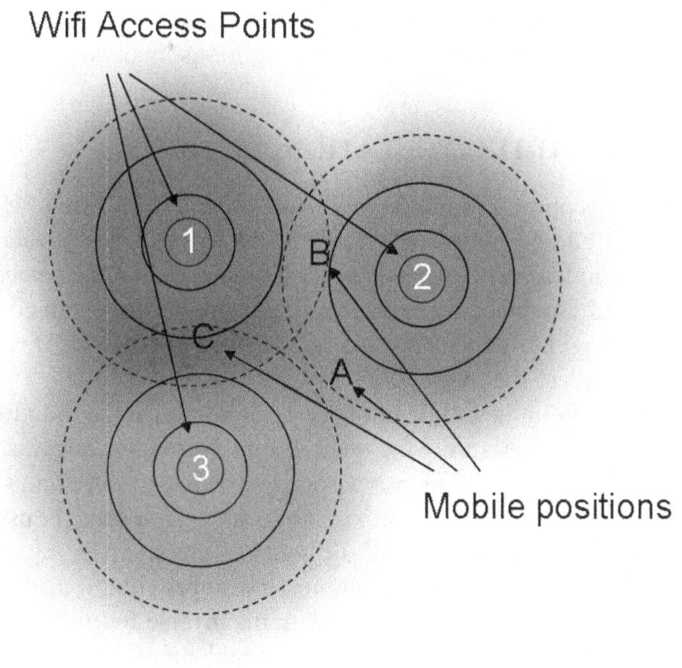

Wifi Access Points

Mobile positions

**Figure 13.4**  The use of signal strengths from multiple Wi-Fi hotspots.

The more complex the placement of Wi-Fi units and the more units present, the better the system will work, minimizing sensitivity to blind spots due to obstructions or the sudden absence of a Wi-Fi unit due to a local power-off condition.

In the "real" world, obstructions present within a space (walls, filing cabinets, etc.) will attenuate the Wi-Fi RF signals more than the ideal inverse fourth law would predict, and so the concept presented above is only a good first guess. It is much better to include a mapping process that must be completed by the system administrator in which signal strengths at various locations within a targeted area are measured and then recorded into a more precise map of signal strengths. The disadvantage of this mapping step is the time required by the administrator to physically map all of the Wi-Fi-controlled environments in which location will be used. However, newer Wi-Fi control systems are beginning to include automatic mapping functions as part of the software, so the disadvantage may be short-lived.

## Wi-Fi Location Attack Vectors

*Jamming*
Flooding a region with strong RF centered on the frequencies used by Wi-Fi access points can have two immediate effects on the operation of a Wi-Fi-based location system. First, sufficiently strong flooding will create a denial-of-service situation in which mobile users will be unable to connect or otherwise maintain connection to a selected access point. Second, such an RF flood can effectively overwhelm the signal strength of any existing Wi-Fi transmitters, erasing the signal-strength map. This causes a user's device to return an ambiguous set of signal-strength measurements that may cause an error in a lookup-table transformation or other inverse-mapping algorithm.

*File Compromise on the Client and Server*
Information about the map of signal strengths throughout a protected area must be stored in a file that is accessible to the server. Compromise of this file can allow an attacker to gain knowledge of the signal-strength map or to replace it with altered and customized information that best suits the needs of the attacker. A more direct attack would require that the attacker gain physical access to a protected space and then store measured signal strengths that are available in the area for later use.

During the operation of a Wi-Fi location system, a user device (a client) must submit information about observed signal strength to the server so that its location can be authenticated. If this information is stored in a file on the user's device, the capture of that file by an attacker will provide

**Table 13.1**    Relative Wi-Fi signal strengths from Figure 13.4.

| | Measured Relative Strengths | | |
| Device | Source 1 | Source 2 | Source 3 |
|---|---|---|---|
| A | 3 | 5 | 4 |
| B | 4 | 5 | 3 |
| C | 5 | 3 | 5 |

valuable information about the signal strengths observed within an operational area. But it is not necessary that this information be stored in a file. An attacker can use a packet sniffer to capture the reported signal strengths as they are transmitted to the server.

### *Spoofing*

Signal strengths in a Wi-Fi location system must be relatively stable in order to be useful for the location-recognition algorithm, and so replay attacks are particularly useful here unless the data packets are encrypted with session keys. Armed with data captured using a packet sniffer that monitored data packets between a client and a server in an area that is protected by Wi-Fi location technology, an attacker can easily spoof the location of his machine by using a replay attack that employs these data packets.

Alternatively, knowledge of the signal-strength map obtained by attacking the map file that is used by the server can also enable an attacker to create a successful spoof attack. In fact, knowledge of the complete map is potentially more valuable to an attacker than captured data packets, since the complete map gives an attacker the means to spoof any location within the protected area, not just the one captured by the packet sniffer.

### *Inadvertent Confusion*

Since structures within the space can attenuate RF signals and directly affect a signal-strength map, changes in those structures can create immediate problems with recognized signal strengths. Movement of office partitions, desks, printers, and file cabinets can all affect local signal strengths and alter the map of all points in the immediate vicinity. Movement of major office items can occur often, and this can cause inadvertent changes to the signal maps, thereby creating denial-of-service conditions for some users until the map is updated. Administrators should be mindful of the possible impact of furniture in a Wi-Fi location-protected environment.

## TIME OF FLIGHT

Measurement of the propagation time of pulses—time of flight (TOF)—that are emitted at regular intervals from any source (local or satellite) could be used in a triangulation system to determine location. The speed of light is approximately 1 foot per nanosecond (a nanosecond is $10^{-9}$ seconds) or 1 meter in 3 nanoseconds. By time-stamping the departure of a timing pulse and using a specialized clock on a receiver that has a precision of a nanosecond or so, it should be possible to determine the distance from the timing source to the receiver to a precision of a foot.

Systems that introduce special broadcasting devices placed strategically in the ceiling of an area to be protected can employ this sort of technique to obtain higher precision that is possible with a signal-strength approach. These devices offer additional advantages over the use of conventional Wi-Fi units for location determination. For example, the specific frequency chosen for the devices requires the use of complementary special-purpose receivers, which might be hard to obtain. The devices can use proprietary protocols, since their function is specific to location. These protocols can use encryption. Finally, software to monitor or otherwise communicate with these devices is (presumably) uncommon and can be protected by password locks or other registration procedures. These advantages make hacking of such systems much more difficult than hacking of Wi-Fi-based location systems.

**TOF Attack Vectors**

The installation of a special-purpose TOF system introduces a variety of additional complications that, if incorrectly executed, can create openings for attacks. The mounting of special-purpose broadcast units throughout an area requires proper attention to visibility and power issues. Line-of-sight obstructions need to be considered for the specific frequencies being employed. Sources of local noise at the selected frequencies need to be identified and adjusted appropriately to optimize the signal-to-noise ratio for the timing pulses.

TOF systems are just as susceptible to jamming and other denial-of-service attacks as signal-strength and geolocation techniques are. Attackers can introduce a noise generator that operates at the specific frequencies of the TOF system, thereby dramatically reducing the signal-to-noise ratio measured by the receivers and creating a denial-of-service (DOS) situation. Alternatively, a broadband noise generator operating at higher power levels can also produce a DOS condition. The TOF server application must properly handle DOS conditions by not allowing access to users that present unusual location data or perhaps no location data. As with signal-strength systems, the map that allows a conversion of TOF data to location must be protected on the server.

**SHORT-RANGE BEACONS**

A simple variation on TOF systems involves the introduction of a proprietary beacon that emits short-range encrypted signals that include time, date, and location identifiers. To the extent that copying or theft of these beacons is prevented by the manufacturing process, the technology can provide simple true/false evidence that a receiving computer was present within range of a specified beacon at a certain time and date. Although not exactly a location system, the short-range nature of the signal allows a properly protected installation to ascertain that a device must have been physically present in order to capture the beacon signals. This can be further enhanced by adding nonrepeating random numbers within the encrypted signal so that each captured beacon broadcast contains a "secret" that is only known by the server and receiving units that have the ability to capture and decrypt the beacon packets. Records of the random numbers that are emitted can be recorded on a server for later validation of a device's presence within the physical space. This approach avoids possible replay attacks by attackers who capture data packets from a user's computer.

## RF POWER SPECTRUM

In any given environment, there is a mixture of electronic equipment (such as PCs, Wi-Fi access points, air-conditioning units, and cellular and cordless phones) that emit signals at various frequencies. To some extent, the specific mixture of these signals and their strength as a function of position is unique. Using a broadband receiver and performing a power-spectrum analysis of the sort described in Chapter 3, it is possible to characterize the noise spectrum as a function of location within an area. To the extent that the sources are stable and predictable (that is, they are not being turned on or off or moved around on a frequent basis), such an RF power spectrum could be used to indicate an approximate location of a device.

### Power-Spectrum Attack Vectors

The very principles upon which RF power-spectrum systems rely are the attack vectors for such systems. Broadband or narrow-spectrum noise generators can distort the power spectrum sufficiently to either alter a device's apparent location or render it unrecognizable, creating a DOS condition. Daily variations in use of equipment can dramatically alter the power spectrum as laptops are brought into a space, turned on and off, and moved about during the workday. As cited above, the map containing the conversion of signal to location must be protected properly. In general, power-spectrum approaches are not considered sufficiently stable or resistant to attack to warrant their use in secure environments.

## RF SIGNATURES

Unlike RF power-spectrum approaches, there is a class of location technologies that employ RF technology to obtain information about passive characteristics (as opposed to RF spectrum tools, for example) of the surrounding space. This environment-specific information has a spatial resolution of about 10 feet (3 meters) and operates in both exterior and internal locations (such as inside office buildings). One such technology, the Location Specific Digital Fingerprint$^{TM}$ (LSDF$^{TM}$) from Digital Authentication Technologies, Inc. (DAT), in Boca Raton, Florida, has been deployed and tested at various customer locations[2]. Using a special hardware device called the Trilobite$^{TM}$ (an early example is shown in Figure 13.5), the technology uses distant RF timing sources at multiple frequencies to extract information about certain types of intervening material that lie along the line of sight. This process is performed over a full hemispherical region centered on the sensing device and creates a map of the surrounding environment.

The map is stored as a highly complex "fingerprint" of a location, which is averaged over time to improve the signal-to-noise ratio of the measurement in each direction.

In operation, real-time measurements extracted by a Trilobite$^{TM}$ at its location are encrypted and sent to a central server. The server then uses various algorithms to compare a submitted signature to a library of previously measured signatures. Using confidence clip levels, the most likely location that matches the submitted data is determined (or none at all, if no match exceeds the clip level). The dynamic range (the number of levels that are digitized in each direction) produces a very large and unique key space (analogous to a retinal scan), which would need to be duplicated by an attacker in order to create a spoofed signature. Careful use of selective, random portions of the key space during a challenge/response process precludes attacks by capturing packets, and the introduction of real-time updates to the tables introduces changes that render such captured data packets invalid for subsequent use.

### RF Signature Attack Vectors

The fact that it is not possible to calculate all of the values measured by this process in a single location means that an attacker would need to obtain physical access to the space for hours in order to capture a similar baseline. However, the technology includes additional checks that involve real-time positional data that prevent playback attacks. Jamming of these

**Figure 13.5** A DAT Trilobite™.

devices is more difficult than with GPS, since this technology requires high levels of noise at the multiple frequencies used by the technology. Applications using the technology must handle the situation of "no location recognized" properly to avoid introducing an attack path through a denial of service. At this time, no attack path has yet been identified.

## IP ADDRESS AND CLOCK SKEW

In his doctoral dissertation at the University of California at San Diego, Tadayoshi Kohno demonstrated the ability to uniquely fingerprint a specific computer for subsequent tracking anywhere on the Internet. By capitalizing on microscopic variations in the manufacturing process of clocks that are used throughout a PC, Kohno et al.[3] demonstrated that it is possible to obtain a unique fingerprint for any PC without requiring any specific action of, cooperation by, or knowledge on the part of the user. Moreover, the group showed that the technique cannot be masked by anonymizers or hidden by firewalls. These microscopic variations in clock manufacturing produces clock skew, which is preserved across any TCP/IP connection. Since each clock-skew fingerprint is unique, it is possible to determine whether or not two PCs appearing on the Internet through different connections at different times are in fact the same physical device. This, combined with tracing of packet routes through an internet service provider, can produce an approximate location of a PC. Kohno et al. reported consistent identification even across thousands of miles and through multiple hops. They reported that the technique works on a wide range of operating systems.

**Clock-Skew Attack Vectors**

At this time there are no known attack vectors for this fingerprinting approach.

## REFERENCES

[1] K. Bullington, "Radio Propagation Fundamentals," *The Bell System Technical Journal*, Vol. 36, No. 3 1957, pp. 593–625, 1957
[2] Contact Digital Authentication Technologies, Inc., through its web site at www.dathq.com, to explore the technology, its deployment, and testing results in more depth.
[3] Kohno, Tadayoshi, Broido, Andre, and Claffy, KC, "Remote Physical Device Fingerprinting," *IEEE Transactions on Dependable and Secure Computing*, 2(2), pp. 93–108, April–June 2005.

# Chapter 14

## PUTTING IT ALL TOGETHER

OVERVIEW

The previous chapters have presented a variety of hardware-based computer-security technologies that can play important roles in protecting information-technology (IT) systems. This final chapter presents a method to make informed decisions about which technologies should be employed in order to produce the most secure system for a given user environment. This method is applied to two example environments:

- A maximum-security environment where the contents of the computer, its authenticity, and the authenticity of the user take priority over anonymity
- A computer system that is designed to provide maximum possible security while maintaining user anonymity where possible

There are many intermediate security environments (such as one that minimizes user interaction or inconvenience) that are not addressed here, but the process described below should remain the same.

## THE CHECKLIST

The more layers of strong protection that are employed by a system, the more difficult it will be to break into that system. Unlike "security by obscurity," which does not work, defense by adding multiple layers of security (also called "defense in depth") does work. The fact is that the more security layers that must be overcome before a hacker can gain access to critical information, the more difficult the execution of a successful attack becomes. The question is: which layers should be added for a specific protection environment?

The configuration of any system that employs some or all of the hardware-based computer-security technologies described in this book requires a careful consideration of the ultimate goal of the system. The following list summarizes the items that need to be considered. The possible security elements that can be applied to a given environment have been grouped into two categories: common elements, which everyone should employ independent of the ultimate protection profile; and specific elements, which are optional items that can be added (or not) depending on the specific security and user constraints. Here is a list of the elements:

**Common Elements**
- Cryptographic algorithm
- Key generation
- Hash algorithm for digital signatures

**Specific Elements**
- Cryptographic coprocessor
- Secure bootstrap
- TPM (trusted platform module)
- Secure memory management
- TET (trusted execution technology)
- Biometric device
- Secure token
- Location control

In order to call the reader's attention to the considerations and decisions that must be made for each of the common and specific elements, such decisions are highlighted below with the term "decisions required."

## COMMON ELEMENTS

Attackers will seek the weakest point in any security system and launch their attacks against that point. To paraphrase an old saying, an IT security system, like a chain, is only as strong as its weakest link. Compromises in the strength of any aspect of an IT security system must be weighed against the benefit that such compromises bring, especially in light of their impact on overall strength. These decisions should not be made lightly. Since the common elements should be employed in all systems independent of specific operational or user constraints, the following items should always be addressed.

### Cryptographic Algorithm

Cryptography resides at the core of any computer-security system, independent of most considerations regarding ease of use. Compromises on the strength of cryptography have a direct impact on all other security functions. Motivation for choosing weaker encryption algorithms might include less processor overhead (CPU utilization) or more compact embedded code for devices with limited storage.

#### *Symmetric vs. Asymmetric Cryptography*

Asymmetric-key cryptography is computationally much more demanding than symmetric-key cryptography of comparable strength. However, it introduces a measure of additional strength by eliminating possible theft of the shared keys used in symmetric-key systems. As explained in Chapter 2, symmetric-key cryptography uses a single key that is shared between the sending and receiving parties. In these shared-key systems, it is difficult to maintain strong security if the system must communicate with others who have not taken steps to protect themselves well against attacks. Moreover, the task of securely sharing the key in a symmetric-key system is fraught with security issues that are addressed by asymmetric cryptography. Finally, the loss of a shared key by an attack on a poorly secured system could compromise all systems with which the victim communicates.

Some of the computational demands introduced by asymmetric-key cryptography can be offset by the use of a secure coprocessor. An alternative approach to taking advantage of the additional security of asymmetric cryptography would involve limiting its use to the most secure transactions, and using symmetric cryptography for any remaining transactions.

Some asymmetric-key cryptographic implementations such as public key infrastructure (PKI) employ third parties to certify the ownership of a public-private key pair. It should be noted that management of keys in PKI can become quite burdensome in large organizations, and the administrative overhead due to suspension or revocation of keys grows accordingly. These can be serious inhibitors in the deployment of some large trust-based systems.

As explained in Chapter 2, attackers with unlimited computing resources can ultimately break any cryptographic algorithm. The single possible exception known at this time is the use of one-time pads. As quantum computing becomes practical, the vulnerability of all cryptographic algorithms will lead to an increased use of one-time pads, which cannot be broken by any computational means. Since they are a shared-key system, one-time pads must be protected during the sharing process to guarantee against interceptions and copies, but proper deployment can produce a strong cryptographic system that is not vulnerable to the increasing threat of computing power. By their nature, one-time pads must be equal to or larger than the message being encrypted, so storage space and the difficulty of issuing additional pads will limit the widespread use of the technology except for the most demanding of secure communications.

*Decisions Required*

- The core cryptographic algorithms (whether symmetric, asymmetric, or both) must be selected. A reasonable implementation would include a mixture of asymmetric cryptography limited to high-security functions, symmetric cryptography for lower security functions, and the use of a secure coprocessor to reduce the demand on the host CPU.
- The precise mix of asymmetric and symmetric algorithms and the presence of a coprocessor must be determined.

**Key Generation**

Good security requires large, unpredictable keys. A hardware-based random-number generator should be employed that uses any one of the physics-based processes described in Chapter 3. Wherever possible, technologies that provide physics-based random numbers along with information about the surrounding environment should be preferred. The key size should be set to at least 256 bits, with larger key sizes selected as a default if possible. Recall that the larger the key, the longer it will take an attacker to break it through brute force attacks. As quantum computing develops, its ability to break cryptographic systems and guess keys will increase rapidly, so early protection is advised.

*Decisions Required*

- The physical process used to create the hardware-based random numbers must be selected.
- The key size must be selected. The use of mnemonics to aid in the recollection of passwords is recommended to improve the ease of use of any user-defined large keys.

### Hash Algorithm for Digital Signatures

Hash algorithms are used to create digital signatures. The two primary desirable qualities of a hash algorithm are: the uniqueness of each signature (that is, a low probability of message collisions) and the inability to reverse the signature (that is, determine the original message based on its signature).

As explained in Chapter 2, SHA-1 has been "broken" in the sense that its attack space has been successfully reduced. Therefore, SHA-256 is a minimum requirement for any secure system using hash algorithms to establish authenticity of its elements or users. Novel or proprietary hash algorithms should be considered with extreme caution, since the validation of their strength requires extensive field testing and mathematical scrutiny.

Hardware modules such as TPM should only be used if they include SHA-256 or later hash algorithms.

*Decisions Required*

- Some versions of TPM employ the "broken" SHA-1 technology. The use of any signature-generating components should employ SHA-256 or similarly unbroken hash algorithms.

### SPECIFIC ELEMENTS

With the selection of the common elements in hand, a user or administrator must next decide which additional hardware security elements should be employed for the specific environment being protected.

## Cryptographic Coprocessor

Cryptographic processes become increasingly important as an administrator or user takes steps to make a system more secure. The consequent increased use of cryptographic processes can place a demand on the system's CPU. Moreover, security weaknesses in the host system's OS can provide attack avenues into the CPU's memory that might allow an attacker to obtain critical key information. Both of these issues can be successfully addressed by using a secure coprocessor to run any security-related processes, store keys, and maintain authentication information about software and hardware components.

Issues of cost aside, a secure coprocessor is well worth implementing on any system that is intended to be used in a secure manner. Its presence will facilitate heavier use of computationally intensive asymmetric cryptography processes as well as provide independence and protection from possible operating-system weaknesses.

### Decisions Required

- Decide whether or not a secure coprocessor will be used. Cost may be a factor. In general, a secure coprocessor is highly recommended.

## Secure Bootstrap

A secure bootstrap process includes the authentication of all of the hardware and software elements involved in the startup process. As explained in Chapter 6, secure bootstrap processes employ a trust-inheritance concept through comparison of current hash signatures from these elements to signatures that have been stored in a trusted environment. Some systems consider only the manufacturer's environment as secure. The benefit of a secure bootstrap process is that any malicious or unauthorized changes can be detected immediately before any damage is done to the integrity of the system's security components.

Because the inheritance concept might begin with the manufacturer, and because a remote administrator might be able to query a system to determine which software and hardware components are being used, certain situations might raise concerns about privacy or the ability of a provider to exclude competition.

### Decisions Required

- Decide whether or not the security benefit of a secure bootstrap process outweighs any concerns about privacy. Moreover, the (remote) possibility that a vendor might employ the technology to exclude the use of competitors' components on a machine should also be considered.

## TPM

As the use of personal computers for online financial transactions grows, more systems are storing sensitive personal and financial information. The failure to protect this information properly has given rise to identity theft and related crimes.

The responsibility to protect personal information resides both with the originator himself (by protecting information on his PC) and with the organizations online that receive and use that information. Protection by using encryption and passwords or biometrics is a good first step, but the encryption keys and the software used to access the information must also be protected.

The increased dependence on electronic networks heightens the urgency for hardware-based protection of information, authentication of users, and creation of high degrees of trust in local and remote computing systems. The economic impact of failure to protect such information is demonstrated almost daily by the loss of private information, identity theft, and hacking.

The system that protects the user's information must ultimately be trusted to behave as the user intends. Once this trust has been established by the use of tamper-evident and tamper-resistant hardware (the trusted platform module), this trust can then be extended outward to the online community at large. Those systems that cannot present evidence of that trust can be treated separately.

A properly designed TPM must satisfy a variety of requirements:

- The TPM must be a hardware device.
- It must check and verify the integrity of the system's hardware and software during the boot process.
- It should provide authentication and status information to local and remote (authenticated) administrators as well as to software programs that request such information.
- It must provide a secure storage location for the user's private keys and private data and give control over these items to the authenticated user.
- It must include strong physical protection (tamper evidence and tamper resistance) so that its contents are protected against physical attack.

- The cryptographic keys that control critical resources (root access, secure memory routines, administration functions, etc.) must be stored within the TPM.
- A true random-number generator would reside within the TPM.
- Associated functions such as critical cryptography, hashing, and the creation of digital signatures or certificates should be performed within the TPM boundaries.
- Data traveling into and out of the TPM should be cryptographically secure.
- It should be not only physically bound to the host platform but also bound through manufacturer-owned signed digital certificates that are stored at the time of initialization at the factory so that swapping of the TPM module would be easily detected.

### *Decisions Required*

- Decide whether or not a TPM will be used. Although cost may be a factor, a decision must also be made about privacy. In the same way that a TPM will establish the identity of the user and his software and hardware with a high degree of certainty in order that legitimate transactions can proceed with confidence, the unquestioned identity of the user is also established for any transactions, whether legitimate or not.

### Secure Memory Management

The need for secure memory management first surfaced when buffer overflows became a useful attack mechanism. As multitasking increased and Internet attacks became increasingly more sophisticated, secure memory management became more of a requirement than an option. In Chapter 7, a list of recommended practices for the developers of applications was presented. The use of these practices should go a long way toward minimizing memory-based attacks.

### *Decisions Required*

- The use of secure memory-management software applications, including operating systems, is recommended.

### TET

Intel recently launched a secure computing initiative initially code-named LaGrande. Renamed the Trusted Execution Technology (TET or TXT), this initiative is Intel's path towards creating a trusted platform. It provides a specification that defines how the TET hardware can be used to extend the trusted platform to include operating systems created by developers that employ the technology. As explained in Chapter 7, developers must be careful to follow Intel's specs in order to maximize the protection and added trust offered by the technology. TET offers enhanced protection in:

- Protected execution: preventing unauthorized applications from gaining access to information belonging to protected applications
- Protected storage: TET uses TPM to encrypt and store keys and sensitive data
- Protected input: TET uses encryption between the CPU and external devices, such as a keyboard, mouse, or USB device
- Protected graphics: TET creates boundaries between applications, protecting frame buffers from unauthorized screen captures
- Environment authentication and protected launch: TET creates a trusted environment using specifications of the TCG
- Domain manager: TET uses a separate domain manager to handle each instance of a protected environment, thereby strengthening the "curtaining" between applications
- Privacy: TET gives the user complete control over whether or not a protected partition will be employed for any given application; moreover, the user maintains knowledge and control over any system trust evaluations that are transmitted over any network

*Decisions Required*

- Decide on a case-by-case basis whether or not the privacy control offered by the TET system is appropriate and acceptable. The TET system employs specific hardware and software applications that require the presence of TET-compatible devices. Cost and compatibility may be an issue.

**Biometric Device**

As described in Chapter 11, there is a wide variety of biometric technologies available today. These technologies vary in cost, accuracy, and ease of use. Some environments may be satisfied with the use of passwords, in which case the creation of long passwords using mnemonics to provide strength is strongly recommended.

Some biometrics (such as a fingerprint reader) offer ease of use—the user simply places his finger on the reader or swipes it across a sensor. The FRR and FAR numbers may be acceptable in lower-security environments, but the additional hurdle of attacking and breaking a system that employs biometrics adds a measurable inhibitor to an average attacker and makes attacking such systems somewhat more difficult over the Internet.

High-security operations can take advantage of iris and retinal scans and can even use these in conjunction with other biometric technologies to create nearly impenetrable systems.

## *Decisions Required*

- For low-security, day-to-day personal-computing systems choose between the use of passwords and some of the lower-cost biometrics available today. Cost and portability may be issues, and the user needs to expect occasional failures to gain entry due to the high FRR inherent in some of these technologies.

- For high-security systems weight the cost, ease of use, and administration complexity of the stronger biometric technologies against the increased security against unauthorized entry.

## Secure Tokens

The computer security mantra "something you have and something you know" is the basis for the motivation to use secure tokens as part of a secure system. RFIDs, smart cards, and interactive tokens all fall into this category. They bring an extra requirement to the authentication process and immediately eliminate an entire class of attackers who do not know how to bypass the token interaction. They are recommended for low and medium security environments.

## *Decisions Required*

- Cost, usability, and lockout are all issues that must be evaluated when considering the use of tokens as part of the user-authentication process. Cost aside, if a token is left behind, the user is either locked out of the system or must obtain some temporary token from an administrator. Some token systems lock users out if they enter the wrong associated password three times in a row. Interactive tokens that change their code periodically occasionally frustrate users when the displayed number changes during the login process, thereby requiring an additional login procedure.

## Location Control

The use of location to control file or system access is a relatively new addition to the computer-security architecture. Location first appeared as a means to provide location-specific information, such as the location of nearby restaurants, hotels, etc. As the rate and severity of computer thefts increased, location began to appear as a means of asset tracking. Digital rights management (DRM) is beginning to consider location technologies as a means of adding location control to access rights. Systems are being deployed to introduce location-based access control for users in a mobile environment. This has also been extended to include location-based information sharing, in which networks of authenticated users can share information based on the location of the participants.

In order for a location technology to bring value as a security enhancement, it should have the following characteristics:

- It must be difficult to spoof.
- It must have acceptable FRR and FAR properties.
- If hacked, it must not reveal anything universal about the user's location (such as longitude, latitude, and altitude).

In Chapter 13, location technologies such as geolocation, Wi-Fi triangulation, time-of flight systems, beacons, power-spectrum approaches, and RF signatures were discussed in some detail.

### *Decisions Required*

Consider several factors when deciding on whether or not a specific location approach will be used. These include

- Ease of use
- The consequence of a user being denied access based on noise in the location system
- The use of an additional device if required (recall that this might be compounded with the use of a token and a biometric, making the overall system potentially unwieldy)
- Cost of deploying the selected system vs. benefit gained
- Ease of use of system administration.

## TWO EXAMPLES OF SECURE IMPLEMENTATIONS

Below are examples of potential implementations of hardware-based computer-security technologies to protect two different systems: a system that will operate in a high-security environment, and a low-security, privacy-oriented system. Note that these checklists are examples only and are meant to serve as examples, not final recommendations.

### High Security Environment

The environment being protected in this section is a high-security environment for an organization that seeks to protect its valuable content. Employees have been notified and understand that their movements and actions might be recorded, and such activities are accepted as a condition of employment.

**Table 14.1**    Example of a high-security implementation.

| Technology | Use Decision | | Specific Device |
|---|---|---|---|
| | YES | NO | |
| Cryptography | ✓ | | AES, elliptic-curve, or quantum cryptography (if available) |
| Key generation | ✓ | | Hardware-based |
| Hash algorithm | ✓ | | SHA-256 |
| Cryptographic coprocessor | ✓ | | |
| Secure bootstrap | ✓ | | |
| TPM | ✓ | | With SHA-256 |
| Secure memory management | ✓ | | |
| TET | ✓ | | With SHA-256 |
| Biometric device | ✓ | | Retinal scan |
| Secure token | ✓ | | Interactive token |
| Location control | ✓ | | RF signature |

## Low-Security Environment with Privacy Concerns

The environment being protected in this section is a low-security PC for a user who has concerns about protecting his anonymity. This user does not want to employ anything that involves identifying himself to the outside world. He wishes only to maintain solid security over his system and its contents while minimizing cost.

This construct provides a straightforward way to architect a secure system that meets the overall objectives of any organization or user.

## CONCLUDING REMARKS

Hardware-based security elements provide the strongest security available today. With tamper evidence, a connection to the physical world, and the

**Table 14.2** Example of a low-security, privacy-conscious implementation.

| Technology | Use Decision | | Specific Device |
|---|---|---|---|
| | YES | NO | |
| Cryptography | ✓ | | AES, or elliptic-curve cryptography |
| Key generation | ✓ | | Hardware-based |
| Hash algorithm | ✓ | | SHA-256 |
| Cryptographic coprocessor | ✓ | | |
| Secure bootstrap | | ✓ | |
| TPM | | ✓ | |
| Secure memory management | ✓ | | |
| TET | | ✓ | |
| Biometric device | ✓ | | Fingerprint scan |
| Secure token | ✓ | | Smart card |
| Location control | | ✓ | |

protection against attackers offered by the difficulty of communicating with the device itself, any security system that relies totally on software remains susceptible to attack.

It is best to use the strongest cryptographic elements possible—the encryption/decryption algorithms should be the strongest available, the keys should be long and random, and the hash algorithm should not have been broken. Be mindful of the strength of asymmetric cryptography and its consequent possible key-management issues versus symmetric-key cryptography and the concerns about secure sharing and protection of the keys. Secure coprocessors should be considered for computationally demanding cryptographic choices.

The next branch point in establishing a secure hardware-based configuration hinges on the use of a trust hierarchy in establishing the authenticity of the software and hardware components in the PC. At the core of this decision is the question as to who exactly determines what is to be trusted? If the manufacturer is to be trusted to make that decision, if there is no concern about the manufacturer possibly excluding competitive products from the trusted hierarchy, and if cost is not an issue, then these components are probably a good idea.

Biometric devices in general add an additional degree of personal authentication that cannot be accomplished by any other means. Those with high FAR and FRR rates should be treated cautiously, since the hurdle presented to an attacker is not as high as those that have low rates.

Tokens add yet another hurdle for attackers but add cost and possible inconveniences or denial of access if lost or left behind.

Location technologies introduce new levels of control but might add cost and complexity. Nonetheless, these technologies have a growing presence in the marketplace.

It is important to recognize that there is no single correct selection of components for optimal hardware-based security. Cost, usability, the nature of the data being protected, and the operational environment all add a degree of customization to the mix of components. The analysis and selection process should be carried out thoughtfully.

Finally, it is important to conduct a periodic review of the chosen security implementation. New attacks and new security technologies are being developed every day. The protection of a system must be considered dynamic and fluid, evolving with time as technologies change and improve.

# Glossary

**ACK**   A signal used to indicate acknowledgement.

**AES**   Advanced Encryption Standard, based on the Rijndael algorithm.

**AIK**   Attestation Identity Keys, used in remote authentication of the hardware state of a system. The AIKs are based on Endorsement Keys and are hardware-specific.

**ANSI Standard**   American National Standards Institute, an international standards organization.

**ARC4**   An acronym for "Alleged Rivest Cipher 4," an unauthorized and unconfirmed implementation of the Rivest Cipher.

**ASC File**   An ASCII text file of a specific format, sometimes used to transmit seed conditions for Pseudo Random Number Generators to remote users.

**ASIC** Application Specific Integrated Circuit, a computer chip created to run a specific algorithm.

**Attack Space** A term representing the mathematical estimate of how many guesses (on average) it would take to find a key.

**Attestation** The reporting of the integrity of a trusted platform using attestation keys.

**Authentication** The process of confirming the identity of a person as authentic.

**Back Door** A hidden access point to the inner workings of a system, usually in reference to a hardware test pin or a software security bypass path.

**Beta Particle** A high energy electron or positron emitted as part of the nuclear decay process.

**BIOS** An acronym for Basic Input Output System, the BIOS is code that runs first when starting a computer.

**Birthday Paradox** Refers to the surprising mathematical result that only 25 or so people are needed to reach a 50 percent probability that two will have the same birthday.

**Block Cipher** A symmetric cryptographic process that operates on fixed length blocks of an input message.

**Blowfish** A symmetric cryptographic algorithm developed by Bruce Schneier that can be used as a direct replacement for DES or IDEA.

**Bootstrap** The sequence of execution steps performed by a computer during the power up process (also referred to as "boot").

**Botnet** A robot network attack that consists of placing a virus on a target computer to enable an attacker to perform functions.

**Brute Force** The process of proceeding sequentially through all possible guesses in order to find the key or password of a system.

**Buffer Overflow Attack** An attack that places the processor in a fault condition by causing a buffer to overflow beyond its allocated space, thereby allowing the attacker to gain access to information.

**CAC** Common Access Card, a smart card used by various government organizations to control access to locations and machines.

**CCD**    Charge Coupled Device, the two dimensional imaging array commonly found in digital cameras.

**Certifying Authority (CA)**    A trusted third party that issues certificates attesting to the authenticity of a person's identity.

**Challenge/Response**    The question/answer process between two remote machines to establish identity by requesting information that only the authentic machine could supply.

**CID Number**    Card Identification Number is a unique number printed on each credit card that is not duplicated electronically anywhere on the card, thereby foiling simple electronic copies.

**Common Criteria**    A standards process by which a company asserts what its product does in such a way that it can be tested and confirmed by a third party.

**CRC**    Cyclic redundancy check used to assure that no bits have been lost during the transmission of data across any type of interface.

**CRT**    The Core Root of Trust is a static portion of code that is used as part of the initialization (boot process) of a Trusted Platform.

**CRTM**    The Core Root of Trust for Measurement is another term for the Core Root of Trust.

**DES**    The Data Encryption Standard is a cryptographic algorithm established by the National Bureau of Standards as the standard cryptographic algorithm in 1977.

**DHCP**    Dynamic Host Configuration Protocol, used by networks to establish communications across networks.

**Dictionary Attack**    A password guessing process that employs commonly used words mixed with numerals and often containing substitutions, thereby reducing the time required to guess in the event that a user has employed such a simple technique in the creation of his password.

**DMA**    Direct Memory Addressing, a process by which applications can gain direct access to memory locations, often creating security risks.

**DNA**    Deoxyribonucleaic Acid, the fundamental building block of life, unique to each person with exception of identical siblings (identical twins, identical triplets, etc. all have identical DNA).

**DPA**    Differential Power Analysis employs advanced electronic monitoring techniques in an attempt to gain information about a smart card.

**DRM**   Digital Rights Management is a methodology to prevent unlicensed copying or distribution of proprietary digital content such as music or movies.

**EAL**   Evaluation Assurance Levels are employed by the Common Criteria process to establish a standard for the level of protection being asserted by a manufacturer.

**EEPROM**   Electrically Erasable Programmable Read Only Memory is a type of memory chip that does not lose its information on power off, but can be reprogrammed when needed.

**EFF**   Electronic Freedom Foundation, a membership supported organization that protects fundamental rights independent of technology. Privacy rights are a big concern at EFF.

**EK**   Endorsement keys are hardware-specific cryptographic keys used in a trusted platform environment to protect and verify the integrity of initial trusted settings.

**Encryption Key**   A string of numbers, characters, or a mix thereof, that is used as part of the encryption/decryption process to protect information. Often called a password.

**Entangled Pairs**   Two photons whose measurable properties are mutually governed by quantum mechanical principles. One member of an entangled pair changes its properties when the other member is subjected to specific forms of measurement.

**Faceprint**   A digital representation of a person's facial characteristics for subsequent recognition by face recognition algorithms.

**FAR**   The False Acceptance Rate measures how often a non-authentic person is accepted by a biometric security system due to noise in the measurement process.

**FFT**   The Fast Fourier Transform is a rapid mathematical process to break any arbitrary signal into its component sine and cosine waves. This is often used in power spectrum analysis.

**FIPS**   Federal Information Processing Standards are standards against which IP technologies are measured for approved use in certain environments.

**Fourier Transform**   The mathematical process of breaking any arbitrary signal down into its component sine and cosine waves.

**FPGA**    Field Programmable Gate Array is an electronic chip that can be programmed to hold specific processing steps, and can be reprogrammed by authorized personnel.

**FRR**    The False Rejection Rate measures how often an authentic user is rejected by a biometric security system due to the presence of noise in the system.

**GHz**    Giga Herz is a unit of a billion cycles per second, and is a measure of frequency.

**GPS**    Global Positioning System uses a constellation of 24 satellites that emit timing pulses toward the earth and enable determination of a receiver's location.

**Hashing, Hash**    A mathematical process that turns any size digital record into a small number which can then be used as an identifier or signature that changes when the source file changes.

**Heisenberg Uncertainty Principle**    A quantum mechanical concept that describes the probabilistic nature of quantum phenomena.

**IDEA**    International Data Encryption Algorithm is a symmetric key cryptographic algorithm developed in Switzerland.

**Imposter Distribution**    A measure of the statistical distribution and variance present in a large group of non-authentic biometric data.

**IPL**    Initial Program Load, the process governing the bootstrap of a computer on power-up.

**ISO/IEC Standard**    International Standards Organization/International ElectroTechnical Commission are standards agencies that seek to establish uniformity in computing products.

**IV**    Initialization Vector is the initial seed used by a pseudo-random number generator (PRG).

**Key Management**    The process of managing multiple user and device keys in a local or distributed computing environment.

**KSA**    The Key Scheduling Algorithm is the secret portion of key generation used by the Wireless Encryption Protocol.

**L1, L2**    The two frequencies employed by the GPS system of satellites.

**LaGrande**    The former name of Intel's Trusted Execution Technology.

**LUT**   A Look Up Table enables the rapid conversion of any number to any other number, and relieves the processor of otherwise consuming conversion tasks.

**Memory Management Attack**   Any of a class of attacks that employ problems with a computer's memory management (due to poor programming) to compromise the system.

**Memory Pointer Attack**   A subclass of memory management attacks that employs weaknesses in memory pointer control.

**Modulo Function**   The process of finding the remainder of the division of one number by another.

**NBS**   The National Bureau of Standards is the former name of the National Institute of Standards and Technology (NIST).

**NIST**   The National Institute of Standards and Technology is a U.S. government organization whose mission is to promote technological innovation and competitiveness.

**NSA**   The National Security Agency is the U.S. cryptologic intelligence agency that sets various cryptographic standards and tests new cryptographic algorithms.

**One-time Pad**   Also called the Vernam Cipher, the one time pad is an encryption/decryption process using a non-reused table of characters (the pad) that are passed through a modulo function with the target text. Both the sending and receiving parties must have exact copies of the one time pad, the pad must be larger than the target data, and each "page" of the pad is used only once by both parties.

**OS**   Operating System, such as Windows, Mac-OS, or Linux.

**Packet Sniffer**   A software application that captures and logs data packets that are traveling across a network, often used to extract information.

**PCI**   The Peripheral Component Interconnect is a protocol standard that sets specifications for attaching an electronics card to a computer's motherboard through a connector.

**PCR**   The Platform Configuration Register is secure storage for hardware measurements made at the core root of trust (CRT).

**Phishing**   A computer attack using social behavior by creating a fake web page that encourages a user to enter valuable personal information such as passwords and account information.

**PKI**   Public Key Infrastructure is a system that employs a Certifying Authority and two or more users in a way that allows users to consult the CA in order to establish confidence in the other user's identity through the use of asymmetric encryption keys and digital certificates.

**Potted**   The physical process of embedding a device in tough material so that any attempt to tamper with the device is easily recognized. Some potting technologies can damage or destroy the protected content, thereby defeating access to sensitive information contained therein.

**Power Spectrum**   A data analysis technique that provides a measurement of the "power" contained in each frequency that comprises the Fourier Transform of the data. The power spectrum is usually used to reveal the presence of heavily used frequencies or other repetitive signatures within the data.

**PRG**   Pseudo Random Number Generator, an algorithm that employs a seed to produce a pseudo-random number.

**Private Key**   The secret key owned by an individual in an asymmetric key cryptographic system.

**PROM**   Programmable Read Only Memory, a non-volatile memory chip where each bit is set by a non-reversible fuse.

**Public Key**   The public key owned by an individual in an asymmetric key cryptographic system. The public key is widely and freely distributed and published, and enables secure communication between two parties when each use their private keys in conjunction with their public keys to encrypt and decrypt messages.

**Public Key Cryptography**   A cryptographic and authentication system based on trust and employing public keys, private keys and asymmetric key cryptography.

**Quantum Computing**   The use of quantum mechanics to produce a highly parallel processor whose computing power grows exponentially with the number of processing elements.

**Quantum Cryptography**   The use of quantum mechanics and entangled photons to produce tamper-proof encrypted transmission of keys and messages between parties.

**RAM**   Random Access Memory, a volatile memory technology used in conjunction with the CPU.

**RC4**   Rivest Cipher 4, a symmetric cryptographic algorithm.

**RFID**   Radio Frequency Identification Device.

**Rijndael**   The cryptographic technology upon which AES is based.

**Ring Oscillators**   An element that can be used to amplify electronic noise as part of a hardware-based random number generator.

**RNG**   A Random Number Generator, unlike a PRG, is based on a physical device or process, and therefore is not prone to problems created using seeds and the possible use of weak initialization vectors.

**Rootkit**   A program to let an attacker take control of a computing system.

**RSA**   Currently the security division of EMC Corporation, RSA has a suite of security products including the popular Secureid token.

**Saccadic Movements**   Natural, rapid eye movements that help the brain recognize objects.

**Secret Key**   The key owned by an individual in an asymmetric key cryptographic system. This key is always kept secret and never revealed or shared with anyone.

**SHA-1, SHA-256**   Secure Hash Algorithm 1 and 256, both certified by the NSA, are used to create hash signatures (short, non-reversible message digests) of files in a security system.

**Shot Noise**   A type of noise that arises from statistical fluctuations in the number of particles carrying information.

**Similarity Score**   The degree to which two signatures (usually derived from biometrics devices) are similar.

**Smart Card**   A credit-card size device with a secure electronic chip imbedded in the body. The chip is accessed through contact or induction, and can carry personal and security information.

**SOC**   System On a Chip is a complete processor with a small, self-contained operating system on board, for use in certain security applications.

**SPA**   Simple Power Analysis is a technique that can be applied to smart cards in an attempt to extract secure information stored within it.

**Spearphishing**   A targeted form of Phishing, in which a fake web page is used to try to trick a user into revealing secret information.

**Spectral Analysis**   Another term for power spectrum, the spectral analysis employs either an FFT or a power spectrum to examine properties of a data stream in frequency space.

**SRAM**   Static Random Access Memory is a form of memory chip that retains its information without refreshing as long as power is supplied.

**SSL**   Secure Sockets Layer is an Internet encryption protocol used to secure certain forms of communications over the Internet.

**ST**   Security Target describes the security properties of the Target of Evaluation (TOE) in a CC process by revealing the steps taken by the company to create the TOE.

**Stream Cipher**   Unlike a block cipher, a stream cipher encrypts characters one at a time rather than operating on a fixed length block.

**SYN**   A term for Synchronize Sequence Numbers. The SYN flag is used in network communications protocol as part of the process used to establish connections between two machines.

**SYN Flood Attack**   A network attack scheme in which a target machine is subjected to a flood of SYN flags. The rate of new requests for synchronization quickly overwhelms an unprotected machine, thereby creating a denial of service in which the machine appears to hang.

**Tamper-aware**   A technology that changes its operational state in response to attempted tampering through the use of non-reversible changes that can be detected by the device.

**Tamper-evident**   A technology that changes its visual appearance irreversibly in response to tampering.

**TCP/IP**   Transmission Control Protocol/Internet Protocol, the communication technology underlying Internet communications today.

**TCG**   Trusted Computing Group, a standards organization dedicated to creating trusted computing platforms, devices that employ trust to establish the integrity of their hardware and software configuration.

**TCPA**   Trusted Computing Platform Alliance was the predecessor to the Trusted Computing Group.

**TET, TXT**   Trusted Execution Technology, formerly called LaGrande, is Intel's trusted platform technology.

**Thermal Noise**   Noise due to the thermal agitation of conductors within a device, also called Johnson-Nyquist noise.

**Thermogram**   An image of temperature regions obtained using infrared optics and imaging technologies.

**TOE**   Target of Evaluation is the security object under evaluation in a Common Criteria certification process.

**TOF**   Time of Flight, a term referring to the time required for a signal or object to travel in a straight line from point A to point B.

**TPM**   Trusted Platform Module is a device that meets the standards set by the Trusted Computing Group.

**Trilobite**   The location-aware device from Digital Authentication Technologies, Inc.

**Triple DES**   An encryption protocol that employs three passes through the DES encryption algorithm.

**Trojan**   Named after the Trojan Horse of ancient times, a Trojan is a virus that masquerades as a normal program. It unleashes viruses and delivers information and control to its original owner after infecting a target machine.

**Trusted Path**   A communications path that assures a user that he is actually communicating with his intended party, and that eavesdropping is prevented.

**TTP**   A Trusted Third Party is a part that can act as an independent storage and confirmation site for secure transmissions between two parties. Secure coprocessors can assume this role if implemented correctly.

**USB**   Universal Serial Bus, a communications protocol and interface for attaching external devices to a computer.

**Vernam Cipher**   The basis for the one-time pad, the Vernam cipher is a stream cipher that employs a string of characters of the same length as the target. The characters are converted using a modulo operation to encode the message. The receiving party must have the same string of characters to decode the message upon receipt, and the messages must be used only once. The Vernam cipher is the only encryption method to date proven mathematically to be unbreakable.

**Voiceprint**   A digital representation of the characteristics of a speaker's voice while saying prescribed words or expressions, for later use as a recognition technology.

**VPN**   A Virtual Private Network is a communications network that operates within the protocols of a broader network (such as TCP/IP). The VPN is usually encrypted and often limited in access to specific authorized individuals.

**WEP Protocol** Wired Equivalent Privacy is a cryptographic protocol for wireless networks that employs strong authentication and large encryption keys to achieve improved protection (as the name implies, equivalent to wired privacy).

**Wi-Fi** The name of a wireless technology protocol owned by the Wi-Fi Alliance.

**XOR** A digital logic element that implements the XOR truth table (shown in Chapter 2).

# INDEX

## A
ACK, 15
AES, 2, 18, 24, 29–32, 39, 210–211
Application Specific Integrated Circuit (ASIC),
 106, 115, 118, 123
Asymmetric cryptography, 2–5, 13, 51, 75, 80,
 84, 120, 122, 132, 201, 202, 204, 212
Attack space, 6, 7, 11, 42, 45, 171, 179, 203,
Attestation Identity Key (AIK), 108
Authentication, 6, 9–11, 14–16, 47, 52, 55, 58,
 62, 67–71, 73, 75–81, 86, 96, 99–100, 104,
 107–108, 113, 118, 120, 127–129, 131,
 137–138, 140–145, 167–168, 170,
 172–173, 178, 186–188, 195, 204–205,
 207–208, 212,

## B
Bifurcation, 154
Biometrics, 10–11, 62, 67, 80, 128–134,
 137–138, 140, 145, 147, 155, 157, 165,
 188, 200, 205, 207–212
BIOS, 84–85, 109
Birthday paradox, 29, 36, 38–39, 43
Block cipher, 18, 24, 28–29, 40
Blowfish, 18, 28–31,
Bootstrap loading, 60–61, 83–90, 96, 98–99,
 106–107, 200, 204, 210–211
Brownian motion, 48–49
Brute force attack, 7, 21, 24, 29, 36, 39, 42–43,
 51, 171, 203
Buffer overflow, 61–62, 90–93, 107, 110, 206

## C
Capacitive scanner, 135, 153
Certifying Authority (CA), 75–76, 132
Clock skew, 140, 142–143, 196–197
Common Access Card (CAC), 174
Common Criteria (CC), 88
Core Root of Trust for Measurement (CRTM),
 84, 106
CRC, 25–26
Crossover, 154
Cryptography
 Symmetric, 2, 5, 19, 21, 24, 84, 201–202,
 204
 Asymmetric, 2, 5, 84, 201–202, 204, 212

## D
Deep Crack, 7
DES, 2, 7, 16, 18–19, 21–24, 28, 59, 118, 175
Dictionary attack, 7, 13, 42, 109, 179
Differential power analysis (DPA), 124, 126,
 176
Diffie–Helman algorithm, 3
Digital Rights Management (DRM), 111–114,
 181, 209
Direct Memory Access (DMA), 64, 87, 110
DNA, 128, 139–140
Dot, 154

## E
Electric field sensor, 135, 153

Printed in the United States
By Bookmasters